MW00779613

TRANSLATED BY EMILE BURNS

The Memoirs of the
CROWN PRINCESS
CECILIE

With 36 Illustrations

LONDON
VICTOR GOLLANCZ LTD
14 Henrietta Street Covent Garden
1931

Printed in Great Britain by
The Camelot Press Ltd., London and Southampton

TO MY CHILDREN

CONTENTS

LIST OF ILLUSTRATIONS

LIST OF ILLUSTRATIONS

CHAPTER I

MY ANCESTRY *NORTH - GERMANY*

The Grand Ducal House of Mecklenburg, from which
I am descended, was closely linked by family ties with
two other ruling houses, the Prussian and the Russian.

As far back as the year 1799 Friedrich Ludwig, afterwards Hereditary Grand Duke, had brought home
to Mecklenburg a Russian Grand Duchess, Helene
Paulovna, daughter of Tsar Paul I; her memory is
preserved to this day in the marble mausoleum in the
park at Ludwigslust. Their son, Paul Friedrich, strength-
ened the link between Mecklenburg and Prussia by his
marriage, in the year 1822, to Princess Alexandrine,
who was the sister of Kaiser Wilhelm I and of the Tsarina
Alexandra (Charlotte) of Russia. The sons of the Princesses Alexandrine and Charlotte, that is to say, the Grand
Duke Friedrich Franz II and the Grand Duke Michail
Nikolaievich, were my grandfathers, so that I am
descended from Queen Luise through both my great-
grandmothers.

A more recent link with Russia was finally to lead to
the marriage of my parents. In 1874 my father's sister
Marie married the Grand Duke Vladimir and went
with him to his home in the north. On one of his frequent
visits to his sister in St. Petersburg my father, who was
then heir to the Grand Duke, and afterwards became

Grand Duke Friedrich Franz III of Mecklenburg-Schwerin, made the acquaintance of the young Grand Duchess Anastasia Michailovna and fell in love with her. In May 1878 he asked my mother's hand in marriage, and three-quarters of a year later, on the twenty-fourth of January, 1879, my parents' wedding was celebrated at the Winter Palace in St. Petersburg, in accordance with the rites of both the Lutheran and the Orthodox Churches. After a succession of sumptuous festivities my father brought his beautiful young wife to his Mecklenburg home.

When they reached Schwerin on the eighth of February, the young couple were welcomed with cordial affection by the town and country population of the Grand Duchy. For my grandfather, the Grand Duke Friedrich Franz II, who was then in the thirty-seventh year of his reign, loved his people, and did everything for them ; and they requited him for it in that they loved him like a father and felt that close ties of friendship linked them with the ruling House.

My grandfather, as the son of Alexandrine, sister of Kaiser Wilhelm I, was to a marked degree friendly towards Prussia, and his whole life, both personal and political, bore testimony to this friendship. Even though Mecklenburg remained neutral in the war against Denmark in 1864, my grandfather took part in it as an individual, serving on the staff of the Prussian general known as " Papa Wrangel." Then in the war of 1866 the troops of Prussia and Mecklenburg fought shoulder to shoulder in the loyal fellowship of arms. In the war against France in 1870–71 the Grand Duke himself participated first in the siege of Metz, where he commanded an army corps ; and his successful generalship in the later battles against the French army of the Loire won for him the commendatory nickname " the victor of Orléans." His confidence in Prussia's leadership found its confirmation in the Hall of Mirrors at Versailles, and until the day of his death my grandfather retained his faith in Prussia. This faith was reinforced by the close family ties which had long united in joy and in sorrow the Houses of Prussia and Mecklenburg. A fresh link was then created by my marriage, and these close ties have been maintained up to the present day. No family festival passes in either of the Houses of Doorn or Ludwigslust without the cordial participation of both. In 1929, on the occasion of the seventieth birthday of my father-in-law, Kaiser Wilhelm II, my brother and I were privileged to celebrate the day with him, whose spirit remained unbroken by all the blows of fate ; and I regarded this as one more ratification of the old tradition.

I did not myself know my grandmother Auguste, who was a daughter of Prince Heinrich XIII (Reuss). She died at an early age, after presenting her husband with six children, of whom four survived : my father, who was the heir to the throne ; two other sons, Paul Friedrich and Johann Albrecht, afterwards Regent of Mecklenburg and subsequently of Braunschweig ; and a daughter, Marie, wife of the Grand Duke Vladimir, who has already been mentioned. My father inherited from his mother his strong personality, his clarity and confidence, his joy in active work for his country and for his family, and not least, his genuine piety. There is no doubt that my grandmother impressed on him the type of spiritual outlook which is characteristic of my family ; my father's up-bringing was completely in accord with her spirit.

Grandmama Auguste grew up in charming Stonsdorf, in the Hirschberger Tal, facing the snow-covered mountain peaks. An active, intellectual life flourished there, within the circle of relatives who as a rule passed the summer in their country-seats in the valley : her Hessian relatives at Fischbach, the Stolbergs at Jannowitz, and her near relatives, the Reuss family, at Neuhof. The women were the determining element in this circle ; it was they who gave it that note of sensitive refinement which also distinguished my grandmother. It has always been a great pleasure to me to find that my grandparents' memory is still loyally cherished among my relatives at Stonsdorf.

My grandfather's second marriage was terminated by the early death of the Grand Duchess, formerly Princess Anna of Hessen-Darmstadt, when her first child, a daughter, was born. Her daughter too died at an early age, when she was only sixteen ; she was worshipped in our family almost like a young saint.

His third wife survived my grandfather by several decades. She was the Grand Duchess Marie, formerly Princess of Schwarzburg-Rudolstadt ; we grandchildren respected her and loved her as " Grandmama Marie."

Simple and modest by nature, she was a reserved and deeply religious woman of outstanding intellectual attainments. Her exceptional delicacy of feeling made her hate intrigue and gossip with all her heart, and she could never believe or even say anything disparaging of her fellow-mortals. She had a deep tranquillity of mind, and was always equable ; she was moderate in everything, and always tried to be just. Grandmama Marie was an accomplished horsewoman in her youth, and even in her later years she was an indefatigable mountain-climber. She looked at Art and Nature with wide-open, comprehending eyes, and she liked to travel with my grandfather on the long journeys which he made, as for example in 1872 when they visited the East, in spite of all the hardships which were at that time inseparable from such journeys. At an early age she recognised Wagner's genius, and until the time of the war, although not a passionate " Wagnerian," she was one of the most faithful visitors to Bayreuth ; she had been present, with my grandfather, at the first festival performances. She had a great liking for amateur theatricals and showed talent both in acting and as stage-manager.

She was devoted to her work for the benevolent societies and institutions of the country, some of which were organised after the war of 1870. She was patron, among other institutions, of the " Marie-Frauen-Verein " in Mecklenburg ; and the great esteem which she enjoyed in her country during her lifetime is preserved in the name of the " Marienhaus " in Schwerin, a nurses' training home and hospital which she founded.

Grandmama Marie had also presented my grandfather with four children : Elizabeth, later Grand Duchess of Oldenburg, Friedrich Wilhelm, who was drowned in a torpedo-boat disaster in 1897, Adolf Friedrich, afterwards Governor of Togoland, and Heinrich, Prince of the Netherlands and consort of Queen Wilhelmina.

My grandparents' Court was composed of members of the landed nobility and military officers. Although it was conducted in the grand style of a princely court, the establishment being modelled on that of the Court at Berlin, ceremonial never stood in the way of culture, nor was there any element of constraint. The encouragement of Art and Science was based on the most sincere conviction, and their representatives were always hospitably welcomed and highly respected. My grandfather bestowed special care upon the development of the Schwerin Court Theatre, the rise of which receives honourable mention in the annals of theatrical history. He set aside large sums every year out of his privy purse in order to develop this repository of German culture and to maintain its high level. Through his three highly qualified directors, Friedrich von Flotow, the composer of the operas *Stradella* and *Martha*, the poet Gans Edler zu Putlitz and Alfred von Wolzogen, he secured the best artistes, such as Hill, Anton Schott and others, whose names bear testimony to the high artistic level of his theatre. Opera received special encouragement at Schwerin. Wagner's works were always presented in Schwerin soon after their production, and

The Valkyries was even secured for its first presentation outside Bayreuth after its première. But my grandfather also desired that the beautiful and precious things which he created should benefit everyone, even his less wealthy subjects ; he therefore had the prices for admission fixed so low that they were possible for everyone. He joyfully made sacrifices from his own means—in this again he was the loyal and beneficent ruler—in order to give artistic pleasures to his children.

The two characteristics which specially distinguished him were faithfulness to duty and fearlessness. When the great fire broke out during the performance in the Court Theatre in 1882, he remained calmly standing in his box, exhorting the audience to be calm and self-possessed, until the last person had left the house, and then he himself directed operations. In this he gave a fine example of intrepidity and consciousness of his responsibility to his people.

The Prussian tradition at the Schwerin Court was so to speak personified in my great-grandmother, the Grand Duchess Alexandrine, who was the sister of Kaiser Wilhelm I and daughter of Queen Luise. My personal recollections of this old lady are, it is true, not very clear, as I was only six years old when she died ; but I have heard so much about her from my relatives and from those who had for many years been intimately associated with her that I cannot refrain from recording the picture of her as it has been shaped in my mind.

After the early death of her husband, the Grand Duke Paul Friedrich, my great-grandmother lived in the

Alexandrine Palace in the so-called Old Garden ; it was a very modest house, but there was an old-fashioned comfort within. Its rooms were full of nick-nacks, brightly coloured glass vases and—a countless number of grotesque china figures, which were always a fresh delight to me as a child when, until long after her death, I was allowed to wander with the greatest reverence through those untouched and sainted rooms. She had left her husband's dressing-room untouched as long as she lived : his military coat, his brushes, the theatre play-bill of the day on which he died were still lying there—all just as if he might come in at any moment. My great-grandmother had passed the greater part of her life in these unpretentious rooms. How often did her contemporaries see this old lady sitting at the window, with grey locks framing her kindly, smiling face ! How often, looking down from her window, did she greet the soldiers returning with drums and fifes from their exercises, how often did she make them feel by this greeting : there is a mother welcoming you home !

As my great-grandfather the Grand Duke Paul Friedrich died as early as 1842, my great-grandmother lived as a widow for fifty years, until 1892 ; the official title " Dowager Grand Duchess " was hers until the end of her life. But in Mecklenburg, where she enjoyed the greatest affection and respect, she was as a rule only spoken of as " Her Highness," and in her old age, as " Her old Highness." She was most generous and warm-hearted, and her kindliness flowed from her intense humanity. She had a very straightforward nature ; she was simple and without affectation, and yet always aristocratic in her bearing. She was cheerful by temperament and humorous, and she kept her hearty laughter up to the last days of her life. She combined a wide knowledge of mankind with a very deep, natural comprehension, and she possessed the gift of clever conversation ; without hesitation she touched the right note even with strangers, up to her old age.

Although she was not tall her appearance was impressive. Her grey hair, turning white, was arranged in plaits over her ears, and over it she wore a lace cap with ribbons. In the evenings graceful little curls took the place of the plaits, giving her a very attractive appearance. On ceremonial occasions the lace cap was surmounted by a great diadem of diamonds, which heightened the impression of dignity conveyed by her whole person.

My great-grandmother used to wear a shawl or a lace scarf over her shoulders. In her mode of dress she preserved the style of the 'thirties, to which she remained loyal up to the time of her death. As a rule she wore black, but after the period of mourning she used to wear grey on days of festivity, and on ceremonial occasions for the most part white. The style of dress which she wore included a close-fitting corsage, which was drawn down firmly, but was not laced, being rather wide ; the wide pleated skirt attached to it stood out a little, as there were small steel hoops—a reminder of the former crinoline—in the petticoat. In her later years she always made use of a stick when walking, even in her room ;

when she was dressed for social occasions the stick had to be white.

At the balls, concerts and dinners at the castle the Dowager Grand Duchess was always the central figure as a matter of course ; she had known the families of the assembled company for generations past, and took an active and genuine interest in what happened to everyone. Every day she had a small circle of guests for luncheon ; in the mornings she used to receive visitors. When she set out on any long journey, and also on her return, there was always a long line of ladies who were intimate with the Dowager Grand Duchess and had established the custom of greeting her at the station.

Following the old usage my great-grandmother had two Women of the Bedchamber, chosen from cultured and as a rule noble families, who were responsible for her beautiful attire and made all necessary arrangements. One Lady-in-Waiting, Fräulein von Schöning, was forty-five years with my great-grandmother and survived her by sixteen years ; many years ago she used to be her faithful companion on her journeys to St. Petersburg by coach or sledge.

The way in which my great-grandmother passed each year was arranged with great regularity. The tiny palace in Schwerin, of which I spoke above, served as her residence during the winter and until her journey in the spring. This journey was often to Baden-Baden, where my great-grandmother would meet our family on our way back from Cannes; the last occasion was in 1891. The summer months were always spent in

Heiligendamm, the seaside resort on the Baltic, which is probably the only one that has preserved its old character of refinement ; it is still, up to the present day, our idyllic summer resort. Before and after Heiligendamm she would stay for some weeks in the " Greenhouse," a little garden house in the garden of Schwerin Castle where one could dream the time away ; her memory still lives in the park there, preserved in the statue made by the Mecklenburg sculptor, Berwald, which many years ago was solemnly dedicated to her in the presence of the Kaiser and the whole Grand Ducal family. Before she returned to her palace at Schwerin towards the end of November, some weeks, from the end of September on, were spent in the beautiful castle at Ludwigslust. The old Kaiser also used to come there every year for the shooting, and then there was always a joyous and festive reunion of all members of the family.

Before the railway was completed, my great-grand-mother made the journey to Heiligendamm in an open four-seater carriage drawn by six horses harnessed à la Daumont. When she arrived the houses were beflagged and cannon were fired in salute. She took up her residence in her own Alexandrine Cottage, which was on a steep bank close under the tall beeches of the Gespensterwald. In her day it was only a little house with a tower which could be seen from far out to sea ; now the house is twice the size, but it is still a charming abode near the wide blue sea, where every year my brother and sister hospitably entertain their relatives and intimate friends. There was many a merry gathering on beautiful summer evenings either at the cottage or in the so-called coffee-room at the Kurhaus or in the colonnade. In warm weather to look out over the sea bathed in the sunshine, and in the moonlight or glittering starlight to stroll out along the path by the sea and sit on the white benches amid the incessant murmur of the waves, was an indescribable pleasure.

So there in her cottage the dear old lady held her " Court," which means that there was a daily pilgrimage of everyone who thought it important to be counted among Court society to the Alexandrine Cottage, to bid good-morning to the Dowager Grand Duchess. After this intimate and quite voluntary little " Court," the donkey-cart would be brought out, guided by a coachman in carmine-red livery who walked by the side, and with a footman in the same livery following behind. Then there would begin a happy hour for those grand-sons or grand-daughters who were privileged to go out for a drive with their great-grandmother. My mother had arranged for this donkey-carriage to be provided, when the old lady began to find it difficult to walk.

Probably nowhere else was it customary for sovereigns to preside at the *table d'hôte*, as my great-grandfather the Grand Duke Paul Friedrich and his spouse used to do at Heiligendamm in the Kurhaus or in the colonnade. The members of the provincial nobility were generally at Doberan with their four-in-hands ; at that time the Court resided there. The custom of eating together was kept up for a long time, as until a few years before the war the Kurhaus was the only restaurant at Heiligendamm.

GRAND DUKE FRIEDRICH FRANZ II AND GRAND DUCHESS AUGUSTE

The close personal relations between the prince and the people of his country always seemed to me to be particularly beautiful in my native land ; these relations had been maintained and consciously tended from earlier and simpler times. There was one custom which probably existed only in Mecklenburg and did not end until the revolution in November 1918 ; this was for the ruler of the land to hold " open house " every forenoon, when he could be visited by any of his subjects, whether noble or commoner, who wanted to consult him in any way or put forward any proposal. The Grand Duke would say in dialect, " Now then, tell me in your own tongue," to encourage a countryman who was vainly trying to get out his sentences in the High German which he had learnt for the occasion ; or to anyone who did not venture to say what he meant the Grand Duke would say in dialect, " Tell me straight what you're driving at,"— and everyone went home satisfied. This unrestricted intercourse in Mecklenburg between the ruler and his people created the most beautiful patriarchal relations that can be imagined.

*

My mother came to her new home when she was eighteen years of age. She was like an ivory statue, delicate and transparent, and at the same time tall and slender and stately in her bearing ; she was possessed of great charm, and was kind and friendly with everyone. She came from the mighty Russian Empire and was used to infinite distances and unbounded possibilities ;

she had grown up amid surroundings in which the idea of " narrow-minded " or " petty-bourgeois " was unknown.

Her father, the Grand Duke Michail Nikolaievich, Governor of the Caucasus, was the youngest son of Tsar Nikolai I, and of the Tsarina Alexandra Feodorovna, *née* Princess Charlotte of Prussia. In later pages I speak in greater detail of my dear grandfather. My great-grandmother on my mother's side, after whom I was named, was the Grand Duchess Olga Feodorovna, *née* Princess Cecilie of Baden, sister of the Grand Duke Friedrich I. She had brought up her only daughter with exceptional strictness, and had accustomed her to submit unconditionally to the will of her mother and of her governess. This principle, even though in a somewhat milder form, was in operation also in my own training. It was characteristic of the small amount of self-determination which my mother had as a girl that although she owned an apricot-tree in the garden at Borjom, my grandfather's country seat, she was not allowed to enjoy the juicy, sun-drenched fruit without explicit permission. The strict training of those days must seem immensely hard to our present-day young people, but it certainly had the merit of shielding the growing generation from weakness of mind, and teaching it modesty, obedience and self-control, without which no one can learn to master life.

My mother grew up in the most happy family surroundings, with a troop of six brothers round her. What pain it must have given her in her last years that not less than three of them were murdered by the Bolshevists in 1918 and 1919 ! As a girl she had lived in the Caucasus, in winter in the government buildings in Tiflis, and in summer at Borjom in the glorious Caucasian mountains. It is hardly possible to imagine what a contrast it must have been for her when, accustomed as she had been from her childhood only to sun and warmth, she had to face the discomfort of a northern winter ! It is hardly surprising that my mother found the raw climate of the north unpleasant, and also that it was not easy for her, for other reasons, to accustom herself to the vastly different conditions of Mecklenburg.

*

In Schwerin my parents occupied the so-called New Town Palace, which was afterwards called the Marie Palace ; they spent three care-free and happy years in this beloved home. Here on Christmas Eve, 1879, my sister was born ; she was named after the esteemed Dowager Grand Duchess Alexandrine.

But this untroubled life was not to be of long duration. Dark clouds overshadowed the fortunes of the youthful family, when my father once more fell ill with bronchial-cardiac asthma, from which he had previously suffered very severely through his whole youth. The doctors insisted that he should spend the winter in a southern climate. My parents therefore went to Palermo, where they took up their residence in the beautiful Villa Belmonte. There, on the ninth of April, 1882, an heir

was born, who afterwards became the Grand Duke
Friedrich Franz IV.

From then on my parents' life was passed between
their Mecklenburg home, where the summer months
were spent, and the south, with Baden-Baden or some
other resort as a resting-place on the way.

In the year 1883 my grandfather, Friedrich Franz II,
died, mourned by the whole country and by his own
people as the father of a country is rarely mourned ;
even the Social Democrats lowered their flags for him.
My father took over the government under the most
difficult conditions imaginable. His whole soul was
bound up with his country of Mecklenburg, and it was
infinitely painful for him, as its ruling prince, to have
to spend several months each year away from his country
on account of his health. The very beginning of his reign
was clouded by the fact that he was unable to make the
journey home for the interment of his father. And not
least in the social sphere his absence created a serious
gap for the Court. The people of Schwerin were like
orphans through the long winter, and though festivities
were benevolently organised by the Grand Duchess
Marie, supported by the Lord High Steward and his
wife, Count and Countess Alexander Bassewitz, the
central point was lacking in the absence of the ruler and
his consort.

When I call to mind what my father looked like, I see
before my eyes the most lovable and kindly being that
has ever existed. He was tall and slim in build, with
beautiful gleaming eyes from which his warm heart shone

forth—that is my unforgettable impression of my father. Nothing could bring me greater pleasure later on than when people who had known him well have told me that I look like him. He had to suffer infinitely much, but never did a word of complaint pass his lips. Unfortunately he died much too early for me still to be able to remember his particular characteristics, but in the course of my further narrative I shall repeatedly refer to him again.

After their return from Italy my parents gave up the Marie Palace and transferred their residence to the beautiful castle of Schwerin. In the autumn my father used to like best to shoot in the magnificent forest of Gelbensande, not far from Rostock, which had been made over to him as his own shooting ground before he took up the reins of government. His stay in this bracing climate of sea and forest always brought a great improvement in his health. Here in Ranger Garthe's house in the forest my parents spent many weeks of the year 1886, so that they could move to the castle at Schwerin just a few days before my birth. I mention this because I have always felt so closely bound up with the glorious Gelbensande forest, my whole life is so deeply rooted in this homely soil, that there must be some mysterious connection the existence of which cannot be denied. On September the twentieth I was born in the castle of Schwerin.

CHAPTER II

IN MY FATHER'S CASTLE AT SCHWERIN

All through my early years I always spent the summer and autumn at home in Mecklenburg, either at Schwerin or Gelbensande, and the winter at Cannes. In the autumn my parents would first travel to Paris, while we children were sent direct to Cannes, accompanied as a rule by Countess Bassewitz or some lady of the Court. Our parents came on later and stayed at Cannes with us until May.

But the country of Mecklenburg was our home. This glorious country with its great lakes and forests, and its splendid, straightforward and loyal people, had our whole-hearted devotion—a devotion which our long absence every year only made more intense. Our home in the strict sense of the word was the castle at Schwerin.

This noble structure with its beautiful gables, oriels and towers, looking far out across the countryside, rose like a castle of romantic legend above the blue distances of the Schwerin Lake. It was our family castle, sacred ground to me and to my family ; my ancestors had lived there a thousand years ago. In the year 1160 my ancestor, Niklot, the last heathen prince of the Obotriten tribe, had been forced by the attacks of the Saxon Count Heinrich the Lion to abandon his castle of " Zverin " ;

he burned it to the ground and fled to Werle, where
he met his death. His son Pribislav was converted to
Christianity. All through the centuries without inter-
mission until 1918 our family lived in the island castle,
which was altered many times by successive reconstruc-
tions. In its present form, a true symbol of the Schwerin
countryside, it is the work of my grandfather, the Grand
Duke Friedrich Franz II. One part of it is built in the
style of the Mecklenburg renaissance, and the other is
after the style of Chambord Castle, under the influence
of our family connections with the Orleans.

The fact that our castle is one of the finest royal seats
in North Germany is due as much to Nature as to Art.
Its position on the lake is incomparable, and its immedi-
ate surroundings on the island are wonderful. Trees of
great antiquity rustle in the wind, and green lawns
spread down to the shore of the lake, where weeping
willows dip their graceful branches into the waters. The
waves lap gently against the banks, and crested divers
dip beneath the surface, to re-appear far out in the sunshine, turning and twisting their slender necks. In the
spring and autumn wild swans fly across overhead, and
the sharp cries of ducks and water-fowl can be heard.
On all sides is Nature, vast and unconfined, such as can
only be found in our northern landscapes ; the bright
light and the vivid colouring give it a brilliance of such
infinite strength that one has the sensation of one's life
being completely drawn up into it, completely merged
with Nature. This feeling of the unity of Nature with
my old home is my most intense sensation, next to the

fond memories of my childhood, when I visit it each year. And although the castle no longer " belongs " to us since the revolution of 1918, my heart always beats more vigorously when I see it. What is transitory may be taken from us, but no one can ever deprive us of the imperishable spiritual ties which unite us with our home.

It was in these surroundings that my childhood was passed. On fine days in the summer picnics were arranged in the beech-woods, generally at the so-called Pumpenkopf. We used to enjoy ourselves there in the merry company of a numerous band of play-mates until evening fell. How beautiful it was, when on our way home we came upon great herds of deer in their feeding places, or saw an old animal with her young as they flashed by over the brown leaves and disappeared among the dark firs !

We derived great pleasure from the outings on the wide Schwerin Lake in the little white steam-launch *Adini*, which was manned by Chief Stoker Henk and Seaman Vitense. We took with us tea and bread and butter, and put in at one or other of the beautiful spots on the lake. One day we would go to the Kaninchenwerder and Ziegelwerder islands, and another to the bluff shores by Görslow ; or we would make the long voyage past Schelfwerder and through the canal as far as Paulsdamm. The engines had to run at half speed in the canal, so as not to damage the banks. Our launch slipped evenly but powerfully past the rushes, in which hundreds of ducks sought refuge. In the summer white water-lilies bloomed there, and strange scents rose from the water gleaming under the hot sunbeams.

The *Adini* used to lie in our boat-house, in the castle garden, which as a child always had a secret attraction for me. From there we would often look out at the many oarsmen who peopled the lake. It was my father who introduced rowing at Schwerin, and when his health permitted he often himself put on his rowing kit and took out a single-sculler, from which he got great enjoyment. In my time the sport was energetically carried on by three rowing-clubs, whose boat-houses were opposite the castle.

In years of drought the so-called Great Rock, an enormous block of stone, emerged from the lake, like a great grey tortoise rising above the surface. White gulls would make a resting-place of it, and many a keen oarsman would land from his boat to walk on the rock which was only visible at long intervals. There were buoys and poles marking the channel in the shallows, and it always aroused lively interest among us children when the gallant Henk included this landmark in his course.

It was particularly delightful when we three children were invited to visit Grandmama Marie at Rabensteinfeld and were given permission to make the trip there by boat across the lake. Our aunt Elizabeth would be waiting for us on the little landing-stage under the beech-topped cliff, and would lead us up the steep path to the house. When we got to the top Grandmama would welcome us at the open door of her writing-room, which lay on the side facing the lake and from which an incomparably fine view could be obtained of Schwerin Castle in the distance. When the weather was exceptionally fine we had afternoon tea in the moss-arbour, a snug little brick house, which also overlooked the steep cliffs, or on the veranda of the large drawing-room on the ground floor, where things went particularly merrily.

What merry times we had there in the cosy family circle ! After tea we wandered round the beautiful park, or raced about in the hayloft over the big cow-sheds, or visited the charming little garden house in the Swiss style which my grandfather had had built for his children. It was all permanently fitted up, with its little kitchen and sitting-rooms and bed-rooms, and had served as a play-room for our aunts and their brothers from the time they were children. This little house is probably the only one of its kind, and acquired a certain fame in the family. On other occasions we made excursions, by carriage or on foot, into the country round Steinfeld, and enjoyed the magnificent beech-woods near the Pinnower Lake, which lay in idyllic surroundings. We used not to come home until evening, filled with the most beautiful memories of our visit to our grandmother and of all the happy little incidents of the day.

*

I could ride from the time I was seven. I had a lovely dappled pony called "Snowflake," because its mane and long tail were white as snow. I used to ride on "Snowflake," kept under control on a long leading-rein by the head-groom Arendt, across the castle bridge and through the garden and grounds past the Faulensee and then often on to the drill-ground, where we could have a regular gallop. It was there too that I once got thrown, as every rider should be.

My governess always followed me in a carriage, which was a great drawback to the pleasure of the ride, because after every gallop we always had to wait for the carriage ; the black horses pulling it would be covered with foam after their rapid trot. But my mother would not relax this rule of etiquette, not even in our Gelbensande Wood which was not open to the public, unless my brother was with me as " chaperone." It was only when the Crown Prince came to Gelbensande and requested permission to take me out for a ride that my mother gave way on this strict rule—there was only good Arendt following at a discreet distance—and we were soon able, as a radiant betrothed couple, to thank her for it.

I also had riding lessons in the Marstall riding-school. The Marstall is a long structure built round a courtyard on the picturesque peninsula of Marstall. The large riding ground is in the middle of it. I always felt a little solemn when I entered the hall and mounted a horse to go through my practice in accordance with directions from the head-groom Arendt, and later also from the riding-master, von Maltzahn. I learnt there how to ride correctly in the volt, full circle, half circle and various other figures. But I never derived any pleasure from riding in the school, for I was always wanting to be out in the open air, in the forest and by the lakes.

Behind the stables there were some small offices in

which hung beautiful pictures of my ancestors' favourite mounts, painted by the artist Schlöpke. After my riding lesson I would walk with my governess through the long stables, in which there were about ninety horses. The carriage horses were chiefly black or dark brown, mostly of Hanoverian stock ; there was also a team of six white horses, besides my brother's personal team of four small coach-horses. There were also pedigree horses in the riding stables. Both in equipment and in driving and riding technique our stables were regarded as in the first rank.

Opposite the stables there were the coach-houses, where innumerable carriages of the Court stood in long rows. There too in their magnificence were the Daumont-carriages and the State and Reception coaches which were used for royal visitors and for the official visits of ambassadors to the Court. There also one could find old hunting sledges and Russian " linieke," which we often used on our excursions—long, narrow coaches with a bench down the middle on which the passengers sat back to back ; they rocked about a great deal and just for that reason gave us children special delight. There too were hunting-coaches of every period and of every generation, coaches without springs such as are still used to-day on hunting expeditions ; in the forest they look extremely picturesque, especially in conjunction with the bright hunting uniforms which are a part of the picture.

The carriages used by the members of the Grand Ducal family were dark blue, with yellow spokes ; other members of the Court used red carriages. The coachmen wore a carmine-red livery with gold braid. It was always a wonderful picture to see the carriages waiting to receive guests at the station or driving through the streets of Schwerin. Since the upheaval of 1918, which also put an end to this old familiar sight, I have only once seen the red livery in Ludwigslust : this was on June 7, 1929, at my brother's silver wedding. It made me feel mournful and at the same time happy to see the livery, which revived all the fond memories of the past.

The Grand Duchesses generally drove à la Daumont, that is, in a four-in-hand with wheel-horse riders and an out-rider. Up to the war my grandmother Marie always drove in to Schwerin in this style, from her house at Rabensteinféld, which was quite close. As a widow she also had a " Nachreiter," a mounted groom who trotted along behind the carriage. My mother had given up this form of conveyance ; already in 1898 she had taken to an automobile for longer drives.

My brother liked best to drive a four-in-hand, which he did with great skill ; as a rule he drove his white coach-horses, which were the fastest, but he also drove the black team. There was nothing that I thought more glorious than when I was able to accompany my brother. Automobiles are certainly very practical and convenient and do in fact meet the needs of our time, but for a drive to take the air, to my fancy at least, they cannot in any way compete with a fine four-in-hand of noble horses.

Among the most beautiful of my recollections there is

also the trooping of the colours by the Flag Company of the Grenadiers. The colours stood in my father's ante-room, and on certain occasions, as for example before setting out for manœuvres, they were taken by the officer of the watch and two men and brought out down the wide Obotriten steps. When they appeared in the courtyard the band played the "Present." I can still hear the sound of it as it struck the walls of the court-yard and came echoing back ; I can still see the grenadiers in service uniform and with their marching kit before the manœuvres, or, when there was a parade, in white trousers and with plumes on their helmets ; I can still see the bandsmen with their instruments gleaming in the morning sun. It was a spectacle whose charm was ever new to us, which on each occasion brought us once more under its spell. It was only when the ceremony of trooping the colours was over, when the troops had marched off to the sound of one of our fine old army marches and the music had died away in the distance, that I and my sister—whose interest in all military affairs was if anything even greater than mine—would leave our posts of observation at the window of the en-trance hall, and for a long time afterwards the music would be still ringing in our ears.

*

In fine weather we liked best to play in the beautiful garden surrounding the castle. There was a beech-tree by the lake, next to an oak, and the branches of these two trees were so intertwined that they looked like a

single tree. How often I used to climb up these, from
bough to bough, hidden by the thick foliage from the
castle bridge ! My girl friends, especially Sibylle von
Laffert, and sometimes too General von Maltzahn's
youngest son, used to take an active part in these climbing parties. Friedrich Karl von Maltzahn, my play-
mate of those days, later on, as Lieutenant-Captain on
the *Mainz*, died a hero's death in the fight off Heligoland
on August 28, 1914 ; he was one of the first of our circle
of friends and relatives who gave their lives for the
Fatherland. There was also a grotto by the lake, which
had a special attraction for us, as it was a particularly
good place for games of hide-and-seek. There was a
statue of Neptune in it, of which only half showed ; the
body was in the water, out of which the sea-god seemed
to be just springing.

In bad weather the gigantic castle gave my friends
and myself opportunities enough for the most exciting
expeditions. On the ground level there were secret corners and corridors and narrow passages through which,
we would crawl, making our clothes and hands dirty in
the process. While we were doing this our heads would
be full of imaginary adventures. Equally thrilling to us
were the castle cellars, where, according to legend, in
the Middle Ages the Iron Virgin used to carry out its
bloody work in the castle dungeons. There was a frame
there, to which five sharp swords were fastened, and this
was linked up with the legend—whether rightly or
wrongly is another matter. These swords, set in motion by
some piece of mechanism, are supposed to have cut up

39

the criminal into several pieces, and the pieces were then thrown into a shaft closed by a trap-door and washed out into the lake. Until the revolution the knives stood in a dark corner of the arms-room ; it was always with a secret feeling of horror that we used to go near them, looking for rust and bloodstains.

Among the series of banqueting halls on the third storey there was a large empty room, the so-called " unfinished " hall. We liked best of all to play there. An old guard-house, which had belonged to our father, with a sentry-box and gun-stands, very ancient cupboards and discarded furniture, and not least a carved pew, prompted us to many kinds of games. It all smelt of dust and mildew, and the bare sides of the room and the cobwebbed outer wall heightened the general impression of mystery. It is not to be wondered at that in this room I was always reminded of the horrible story which our nursery-governess had told us.

There was a wedding-feast in an old English castle. The wedding guests were in a boisterous mood, and after other pastimes they finally began a game of hide-and-seek. After a long and merry hunt in every nook and corner of the ancient structure, all the players were found—except the bride. They searched for her everywhere till late in the night, but with no result. The bridegroom and the wedding guests were overcome with horror. Had the fair bride been carried off by robbers ? Had she perished in some subterranean dungeon ? Neither bridegroom nor guests ever knew the answer to these terrible questions. But when, four generations

GRAND DUCHESS ALEXANDRINE OF MECKLENBURG-SCHWERIN,
née PRINCESS OF PRUSSIA

A DRIVE IN THE DONKEY CARRIAGE

later, once again a merry party was romping through the castle, playing and jesting, one of the guests lighted on an old oak cupboard. It was locked, but the secret lock yielded to the chance pressure of a finger, and the cupboard door sprang open. The guest fell back in horror : leaning in a corner of the cupboard was a skeleton, clothed in a white satin dress which hung in rags from the bones, and with a myrtle wreath on its grinning skull ! They hunted in the archives, and there they found a chronicle containing the tragic story of the vanished bride.

Fortunately we never made such a ghastly find, but our childish imaginations were naturally often filled with ghost-stories, especially as " Little Peter," the dwarfish spirit of the castle, was supposed to make his rounds in the castle. It is true that he was reputed to be a good spirit, but nevertheless he was said often to have appeared as a warning of the death of some member of our house. For many long years, however, Little Peter has not been seen, and only a statue in a niche in the castle courtyard still preserves for him a certain continued existence in the memories of the people of Schwerin. There was another legend attached to the " unfinished " hall already mentioned : it was that if ever this hall were completed, it would bring great sorrow on the Grand-Ducal house. When the castle was partly burnt down by fire in the year 1913, my brother, who did not share this superstition, decided to transform the hall into a number of guest-rooms. But before the plan could be carried out in its entirety the war broke out in 1914, and in 1918 our House lost not only the country but also the castle.

Our expeditions in the castle often brought us to a corner behind a little staircase where, as far back as I can remember, there was a beautiful model of a locomotive with a luggage-van and a passenger coach, which had been given to our grandfather in 1865 as a memento of the construction of the Friedrich–Franz Railway. This charmingly fashioned miniature railway train was always an object of the greatest admiration ; we would have been only too glad to play with it and let our dolls make journeys in it, but to our sorrow this was not allowed.

Close by it there was a door, which when opened usually let in a strong draught. If one went through it one stood under the gilded dome over the main entrance, in a space which was open at both sides, towards the courtyard and to the front. On the outer side there was the equestrian statue of our ancestor, Niklot, prince of the Obotriten, attacking a wild ox with his spear ; the memory of those battles is still preserved by the bull's head on our coat of arms. Our ancestral seat was the " Michelenburg," in Low German " Mecklenburg," that is, the Great Castle ; like the castles of all the princes of that epoch, it was built on a hill surrounded by marshy ground. To this day I experience quite a curious sensation when, driving along the road from Wismar to Schwerin, I pass on the left hand, near the present village of Mecklenburg, the wooded hill which can still be recognised quite clearly as the mound of Wendenburg, our ancestral fortress.

When we had explored all the hidden corners of the castle we would come to the halls and banqueting-chambers, walking now on the parquet flooring, polished as smooth as a mirror, through the Golden Hall, where Court balls and concerts took place, through the Wilhelm room, where the Court was held on the occasion of a wedding or other festivity, on into the Ancestors' Gallery and thence into the Throne Room. In the Ancestors' Gallery some of my forebears looked down at me with a threatening look in their eyes, so that I was glad when I did not have to pass them by myself. Later on, my brother and sister used to hold their New Year receptions and military Courts in the Throne Room ; smaller balls were also given there.

My nurseries, which were on the ground floor, had a clear view of the lake. Various short flights of steps led down to a terrace ; but more than once, " because it was simpler," I climbed out through the window and over a trellis that was fixed in front of the cellar windows. Under the wall of the terrace there was a tall fountain, whose jets kept a ball up in the air. In the evenings, before I fell asleep, which I always found it very difficult to do on bright summer evenings, I heard the steamers tooting, ducks crying, and nightingales singing among the old trees of the castle garden—sounds of the far-off time of one's youth which one never forgets !

Two narrow winding staircases led up to my parents' rooms, which were over my rooms. One of them led from my bedroom into my father's large and comfortable writing-room. A thick, soft carpet softened the

43

sound of footsteps, deep divans stood round the room, and there were albums and family records on the tables. A marble copy of Mama's hand, a veritable work of art, ornamented the writing-table, while a bronze image of Papa's hand lay on Mama's table. The wall was decorated by a beautiful picture of my grandmother, Auguste ; my aunt, the Grand Duchess Vladimir, inherited it afterwards, and so it found its way to St. Petersburg. Behind the writing-table there was a marvellously beautiful marble bust of my mother, the work of the Mecklenburg sculptor, Josef Kopf—and this too had its counterpart in a bust of my father which was in my mother's writing-room.

Between the two writing-rooms, or " cabinets " as they were called, there was my parents' joint bedroom, in which I was born. Opening out of this room, in a tower, there was my mother's comfortable dressing-room, which I could reach by one of the two winding staircases mentioned above, which also gave access to Mama's garderobe.

It gave me the greatest pleasure when I came in time for Mama's toilet and, like a true little daughter of Eve, was allowed to admire her beautiful dresses and lace and furs. My mother had an exquisite taste in dress ; as a rule the clothes she wore were extremely simple, preferably white, and she made very little use of jewellery ; she liked best to wear only pearls. With her dark hair, smoothly combed back, and her stately figure, she was an object of unlimited admiration to me from the time when I was quite small. A little story which the old

Colonel-General von Plessen told me shortly before his death shows that I was not the only person who had this feeling of admiration for her. The incident took place soon after my parents' marriage, when they were spending a few days at the Court of Kaiser Wilhelm I. One morning Moltke came to have audience of his Imperial master, and the General Field Marshal's expression was noticeably preoccupied. When the old Kaiser asked him to what his preoccupation was due, Moltke answered " Your Majesty, the young Grand Duchess of Mecklenburg must bear the blame. I cannot help thinking all the time of her radiant beauty ! "

In my recollections of my childhood I still always see Mama in this radiant beauty. The passage of the years made her features a little sharper and her skin a little greyer in tone, but she kept her erect, stately carriage, so that up to the end everyone felt that she was a princess born. By nature my mother was very serious and reticent ; she had probably developed it as the result of my father's long illness and the many afflictions she experienced throughout her life. But how glad she was to give happiness to others ! How happy and content she would be, for example, when we journeyed to Russia and she could see what joy the journey gave me, and how greatly I liked being in the country where she had lived as a child ! In such circumstances she could be almost merry. One quality of hers which was particularly valued was her undeviating loyalty towards all those who showed loyalty to her. No doubt to many she seemed unapproachable, but she only gave this impression when she felt that she was misunderstood. To all her tried friends Mama always showed the greatest affection and constancy.

Once more I pass in spirit through the familiar rooms of my childhood, and reach my mother's immense salon, probably the most beautiful that I have ever seen. It was over the entrance to the Black Staircase, and it had three great double windows overlooking the castle gardens. It was about 16 metres long, and was approached by the Sylvester gallery. Entering from this door, one gained the impression of a vast room of harmonious proportions and with a certain stateliness, which was, however, softened by the many comfortable corners and groups of furniture. On the marble walls there hung a magnificent portrait of Catherine the Great and two delightful pictures by Matthieu, the "Mecklenburg Pesne," portraying the Grand Duke Friedrich Franz I and his sister. Precious snuff-boxes were arranged in glass cases. A gilded sedan-chair of the rococo period used to carry my fantasies back to the people of old times who, in hooped petticoats and powdered hair, had been carried in this charming golden cage to make their visits.

My mother as a rule had tea in the salon when she was receiving guests, and after these ceremonial receptions the family used to gather there, so that the room had seen many an intimate and merry gathering. Next to it was my parents' dining-room, on the walls of which hung costly Gobelin tapestries. When the great fire broke out in December 1913, my sister-in-law, the Grand

Duchess Alexandra, showed great personal courage and coolness in attempting to save whatever could be saved. It was only when the terrific heat drove in the double-doors which cut off the Black Staircase from the Sylvester gallery, and the stairs close by where she was standing collapsed, sending up a thick cloud of smoke and sparks, that my sister-in-law was obliged to abandon the work of salvage. Months afterwards, when I visited Schwerin, there was still one charred beam in the beautifully painted ceiling of the salon—a sight which, in this spot so full of tender memories, I found deeply moving.

In the great tower there was the Flower Room, with tall windows looking out over the lake and the castle gardens. In the summer we generally had our meals here when the family was by itself or there were only a few guests. Green palms and ferns stood by the french windows and round two fountains which on hot days cooled the air. The middle door opened on to the highest of the many terraces which were linked together by a broad flight of steps leading down into the castle gardens.

But the Arms Hall too was often used for meals. It was a splendid room with a vaulted ceiling in which a magnificent array of weapons was kept ; precious old coats-of-arms and mighty antlers hung on the walls, and armour and weapons of every variety were ranged there. In summer we would step out from the hall into the garden, where we could converse with our guests in comfort over coffee. On cold days and in the evenings we would sit by the cosy open fireplace in lively conversation or at a game of cards.

My tour through my father's castle, which I am carrying out in spirit, leads me now through the so-called "church passage" to our dear castle chapel, where I was baptized and confirmed.

Extraordinarily beautiful memories are connected in my mind with going to church. I always sat in the same seat, directly on the left of the entrance to the Court pew. On summer days the sunbeams poured like liquid gold through the brightly-coloured altar window, in front of which stood the snow-white marble figure of Christ. I can still hear the voice of Pastor Wolff, the senior chaplain of the Court, and I can still see the sharp profile of his venerable head rising from the pulpit against the light. My heart was filled with a feeling of infinite solemnity which made it receptive to the Word of the Lord. I still have a feeling of regret that my marriage did not take place in our chapel at the castle, but the tradition of the Prussian Court, according to which the marriages of all Prussian princes must take place in Berlin, made this impossible. My sister was married at Cannes, owing to the Court being in mourning for my father's death ; and my brother at Gmunden. To none of us three, therefore, was it given to celebrate there the most beautiful church ceremony of our lives.

But one marriage which took place in the chapel of the castle has remained among the vivid recollections of my childhood. This was the marriage of my aunt, Duchess Elizabeth, to the Grand Duke of Oldenburg,

GRAND DUCHESS MARIE OF MECKLENBURG-SCHWERIN,
née PRINCESS OF SCHWARZBURG-RUDOLSTADT

which was celebrated at Schwerin in the autumn of
1896. I was then ten years of age, and one thing which
specially impressed itself on my memory was the awning
which was erected from the Obotriten steps through the
courtyard to the chapel door ; the stately procession of
wedding guests walked under this awning, on a red
carpet, to the chapel. Unfortunately I fainted during
the ceremony in the chapel, a mishap which frequently
befel me at church ceremonials when I had to stand ;
and I was therefore quickly put on a bench in a niche.
The Kaiser was present at the ceremony, and also the
Princess Feodora of Schleswig-Holstein, the Empress's
sister, afterwards the " Aunt Feo " whom we so deeply
loved.

Leaving the castle chapel, I go in spirit to the lofty
towers of the castle. Although it was very seldom that I
climbed up to these, the ascent up the innumerable
steps, and the glorious views out across the wide lake to
the distant beechwoods, have remained in my memory
as infinitely impressive. In one of the towers there was
the castle clock, and the higher one mounted the louder
its works sounded. It seemed to me that I was listening
to a giant's heart beating, and I was often seized with a
great dread that I might reach the top at the time when
the hour would strike and be condemned to stand under
the clock and let the mighty strokes fall menacingly on
my ears. From down below, however, the ticking and
striking of the clock sounded inexpressibly mysterious
and intimate ; its familiar sound is one of the dearest
recollections of my childhood. I heard it strike when I

was going to bed and when I was rising, at play and at
work, and at all the merry or serious festivities held in
the castle ; it was the accompaniment of my activities and
thoughts from my earliest days up to the time when, as
a bride, I set out for my new home.

The castle clock still goes on striking above the de-
serted castle, as if it is seeking to keep watch over the
memory of the life that once passed within its walls. May
the Lord God bless its devoted vigil !

CHAPTER III

GELBENSANDE

When the traveller who is making his way along the
road from Rostock to Ribnitz has passed the neat little
station of Gelbensande and has left behind him the last
houses of the village, he will notice, just where the wood
begins, eight white stones which mark the end of a carriage road leading out of the wood. And he will also see
a simple wrought-iron gate which is very seldom open.

For myself and for my brother and sister this gate was
the entrance to our earthly paradise from our childhood
up. The carriage road coiled like a snake from the gate
through the quiet green pinewood. The air was full of
the aromatic odour of the pine-needles, and one could
breathe more deeply in the bracing atmosphere of the
forest. The road was bordered on both sides by oaks,
whose planting we can still recall ; for many years now
they have given cooling shade on hot summer days.
Passing from the dusty glare of the high road into this
peaceful wood, one feels as if translated to another
world, it is all so quiet and homely. Then when one
rounds a corner, in a clearing in the wood the reddish
hunting-box with its characteristic black timbers comes
into view ; this was our most prized home from the time
of our earliest childhood. To me this charming house
has remained up to the present day the home of my heart.

Raging storms have swept over my inward and outward being, my soul has been shaken by happy and sad experiences, people to whom I was closely attached have been torn from me, my riches have been scattered, a world-upheaval has burst upon us—but, God be thanked, Gelbensande is to me still the homely, peaceful refuge which I knew of old. Every year I still go there to find new strength for the tasks which fate has laid upon me.

It is not only the recollections of our happy childhood which always draw me and my brother and sister back to Gelbensande—the marvellous country is an irresistible attraction in itself. On the Riviera we have always enjoyed the views of the southern Alps and of the sea—views which have awakened in us the appreciation of the magnificent beauty of Nature, which can perhaps be called classical. But here in quiet Gelbensande an even more valuable gift was granted to us : the love for what perhaps can only be given by the German forests with all their poetry and inward life.

A wide landscape may make one feel heroic, but a German forest moves one to contemplation and reflection. How infinitely fine and delicate is everything that our eyes see, everything that sounds in our ears, scarcely perceptible, difficult to reproduce, and yet moving the soul like the faintest touches on the strings of an instrument ! Here a German feels nearer to God than anywhere else, here he senses the eternal breath of the Creator, and here he feels closer to the good and the pure than amid the bustle of the towns.

The beautiful hunting-box stands in the middle of the

wood. It was tastefully built by Möckel in accordance with my parents' plans, and they felt happier in this house than almost anywhere else. For here in solitude they could live undisturbed the simple family life which they loved. Every summer and autumn they spent several months with us in Gelbensande. Their only company was a few dear relatives and friends who were invited to stay with us regularly year after year.

The Gelbensande forest has a great variety of trees. Magnificent beeches alternate with lofty pines, and dark firs are next to alders. Among them are scattered single oaks, whose mighty crowns spread like a screen over the younger trees. A narrow footpath, made many years ago, was my favourite walk. It was easy and effortless to walk over the springy woodland soil, and there was a constant succession of the finest views of groups of trees, of ferns as tall as a man, of bushes and herbs ; in the more open spaces the sun flooded the green moss with shimmering light, and new visions were constantly charming the eye. My path led me past a wide brook ; in our childhood we called it the " Congo," and we used to like best to play by it. There too in after years our children in their merry games have essayed many a bold jump across the water.

Beyond this the path led close past a conical hill which is said to have been a barrow, or, as legend has it, a fortress of the famous pirate Klaus Stortebecker. Although several attempts to dig for treasure there met with no success, the hill gave us nevertheless the opportunity for daring climbing parties. Further along this path through the wood one came across three simple benches at considerable distances from each other— each bench was dedicated to one of us three children. The name of the former " owner " was carved in the tree against which the bench leaned. I often sit there on my bench under the glorious old beeches, and think again of the happy days of my youth or try to work out the tasks and problems of the present. There in the deep silence of the wood, with a feeling of absolute security, I reflect on my innermost feelings and thoughts. There too I hold converse with Nature, with which I am indissolubly united. And often the feeling comes over me that I too am a tree whose roots have sunk into the life-giving soil of my home; I feel so intimately intertwined with the magnificent old beeches and pines. How often there in the wood silent but fervent prayers have risen to the Creator of this wonderful Nature : prayers for strength to perform everything in accordance with His will, prayers for still firmer and still deeper faith, to prevent me from deviating or becoming weak and losing courage. I always come back to the comfortable house full of inward consolation and with peace in my heart, after such lonely wanderings through these long-known and unaltered haunts of my childhood.

As my old bench decayed with the years, a few years ago my dear brother and sister had a new one put near it, which is so long that now I can sit on it with my six children. I was deeply moved by this surprise and the effort made by my brother and sister, which expressed itself in this way, to preserve my home for me as I had known and loved it from my youth up. The valet Ihde, who many years before had carved our names over the benches, also cut my christian name and the year in the bark of the beech-tree behind the new bench.

It was glorious for me as a young girl to ride with my brother through the wonderful wood in the early morning, along the charming glades and past constantly alternating plantations. How beautiful it was, especially on clear autumn mornings, when the rays of the sun came slanting down through the beech-tops to the ground, and the freshly-fallen leaves were lit up with a reddish gleam ! The beech-tops flamed in the sunlight and the yellow leaves trickled down like golden rain on to the path, which made a dull vibrating sound under the hoof-beats of our horses. White clouds were sailing above us in the blue ; a buzzard, hovering in the air with outstretched wings, uttered its sharp cry. How nice it was to gallop along the straight roads, and how happy we were after a fast gallop to pull up our horses and, while we were getting our breath again, to enjoy all the magnificence which Nature offered us ! What memories are still attached to every part of that vast forest ! How often we say, " Do you still remember . . . ? " Often they are mere trivialities, but for us they are full of significance because of our common recollections.

In addition to my riding horse there were two small carriage horses at my disposal. As I liked driving myself, it gave me the greatest delight to be able to drive through the beautiful woods with my governess. But these carriage drives did not always pass without accident. Once I took a corner too sharply, so that the carriage tilted over very much to one side, and my governess, who was sitting next to me, rolled out of the carriage ; but luckily she fell softly and did herself no harm. The other occasion was when I made a miscalculation and brought down a post ; the horses were startled by the sudden check, and they began to pull wildly. This made the carriage start a see-saw movement, and Madame Popoff, a rather elderly and corpulent Russian lady, and my friend Marie von Malschitzki, who were both on a visit and had entrusted themselves to my skill, flew out in a high curve. I was, of course, extremely alarmed and anxious over what had happened to my two passengers, but by good luck they too had not been hurt. But Madame Popoff's reproving " People who can't drive shouldn't try to ! " stayed in my mind for a long time, and from then on I avoided dangerous corners so as not altogether to lose my reputation as a charioteer.

Happy recollections of my childhood also centre round a team of two fat cream-coloured Russian ponies which Mama used to drive from a low basket-carriage. It was a very great pleasure to us children when we were allowed to go out with her in this. The fat little horses trotted gallantly along the roads through the wood, trying to keep the flies off with their short-cropped tails.

As a rule the place to which Mama drove was the Hirschburger ranger's house, which lay in a delightful position at the end of the wood, from which there was a wonderful view of the old town of Ribnitz. There, as long as I can remember, lived Ranger Wendt and his

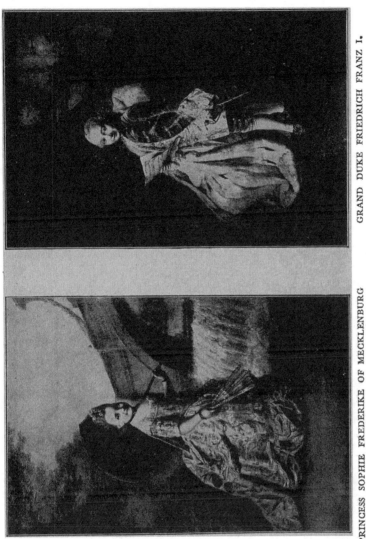

PRINCESS SOPHIE FREDERIKE OF MECKLENBURG
From a painting by Matthieu

GRAND DUKE FRIEDRICH FRANZ I.
Portrait by Matthieu

little wife, who generally had one of Mama's fox-terriers *en pension*. Ranger Wendt is among my oldest and dearest memories of Gelbensande. Tall and of erect military bearing, which he kept until his old age, with gleaming eyes and with a full beard framing his face, he would be standing in front of his house, in his smart Mecklenburg ranger's uniform, when we arrived, and he would greet us with genuine pleasure. He was very well-read, and he liked to discuss serious questions about life. The good Wendt died some years ago, and we miss him very much when we drive to the shoot, and he is no longer at the spot where he used to tell my brother that a good stag had come out into one meadow or another or had been heard in the covert. It sometimes seems to me as if his spirit is still hovering over his loved Hirschburger preserve, where for so long he lived and served his master with unfailing loyalty !

What pleasure it always gave me to drive with my brother or my mother to the great green forest fields where my brother used to shoot ; and even now one of my finest experiences is to go out in the autumn to a shoot by Heiligen-Höhle. When we go out early in the morning before the sun is up, and drive in the half light through the sleepy forest, we can hear the startled cries of the little screech-owls and see the daylight gradually pushing back the deep curtain of darkness above the trees. With the utmost care we leave the hunting carriage and walk cautiously along a narrow path, through the dewy grass and the tall ferns, until we reach the wide field where we have already heard the stags calling. We remain standing there for some time, to see where the game is and from what quarter we can get still nearer up-wind. My brother, who is a good but also a very cautious shot, searches round carefully for the best point from which to shoot. While he makes his way along by himself, so as not to disturb the quarry, we others stay in a little shelter made of branches, keeping a keen eye on the stags with the aid of binoculars. As a rule we do not have to wait long ; the shot rings out, and the red deer and the smaller stags rush headlong away while the powerful fourteen-pointer, hit in accordance with all the rules of the woodman's craft, sinks to the ground. It is true that sometimes we did not succeed in getting a shot so quickly. Particularly in the marshy ground of the Ribnitzer Wood, near the sea, where it is not possible to see far, we often had to have a long hunt with a fatiguing stalk over the uneven ground, and sometimes we came home without having had any luck at all. But we were always richly compensated by the overwhelming beauty of the scenery.

Some of the fields, by the way, have names whose origin must probably be sought long ago in the Middle Ages. Thus for example the names " Mörderkuhle " (Murder-pit) and " Totenbruch " (Dead Man's Swamp) undoubtedly refer to some horrible murder which took place in the dense primeval forest. And again, the name " Heiligen-Höhlen " (Saints' Caves) takes us back to a hermitage where probably the monk Augustin, whose name is borne by the adjoining wood " Augustin's-Horst " (Augustin's thicket), lived a holy and

58

God-fearing life. The little station " Schwarzenpfost "
(Black-Post) on the Ribnitz–Rostock line can be
proved to be the place where once the rich merchant
Wullebrassen was attacked and slain.

My father too had been a keen hunter, and by many
years of care had built up a first-class red-deer preserve
there in the Gelbensande forest. He used to hunt as often
as his health allowed. He was generally accompanied
by Ranger von Oertzen, who, thank God, is still at his
post as fresh as ever up to the present day.

How often Herr von Oertzen has told me of their
hunts, and how I always like to hear him talking of my
dear father, who was so early taken from us ! Papa must
have had an indescribable affection for his beautiful
forest. And how his eyes must have lit up when he had
brought down a sturdy roebuck or a good stag ! But on
these excursions they used also to speak of deep and
serious things, and to this day Herr von Oertzen speaks
with emotion of how near to each other they had come
on such occasions. From him too I learnt how kind my
father was to all around him, and how he smoothed out
every difficulty that arose. Papa, he told me, was always
just to all his subordinates, and willingly helped them
out of any trouble, even when the person concerned had
perhaps unwittingly done something for which he might
have been blamed.

. I was linked with Frau Dagmar von Oertzen by the
ties of a sincere friendship, until God called her to Him
last year after a life that was full of activity. The three
Oertzen children, Karl, Marie, and Anastasia, the

59

last-named a god-child of my mother, were my playmates at Gelbensande both in rambles round the neighbourhood and in the visits I paid to the ranger's house. These generally finished up in the pig-sty or in the hay-loft.

Every Sunday we used to attend divine service in the village church at Volkenshagen. When I was a child we used to drive there in a carriage ; the way led first through the wood and then by roads through the fields over deep scrunching sand. It was a regular expedition, and it took the whole forenoon. Now we reach the church by motor, which is much quicker and more comfortable, but much less poetic than our early carriage drives. Only a year before his death, when the church was being renovated, my father presented it with beautiful altar-windows, which bear his and our names as donors. I still have a clear recollection of the ceremony of consecrating them, when we children walked in solemn procession with our father round the church.

How I enjoy even now going to divine service in the little church ! We still sit in the same pew opposite the pulpit, with everything just as it was then. Even the great black board on which the name of every pastor has been inscribed for the last four hundred years, is still hanging in the same place, and even to-day my eye glances now and then during the sermon across at the names, which look strange enough in their Latinised forms ; only the names of the more recent pastors are there to be read in good German.

But there is also much that has changed. It is not only that the organ no longer has the same squeaking sound as it used to have ; it is not only that the boys' choir no longer sings as much out of tune as before—but even the old black hats of the peasant women, sad to say, are more and more rapidly disappearing, and the old costumes are giving place to more fashionable dresses. The old men with bald heads and fishermen's beards who used to sit on the right on the men's side, while the women took the left side of the church, are long since dead, and a new generation has taken their place.

The old custom, too, for the congregation to enter the church only when the first verse of the hymn is sung, no longer exists, nor the practice of the pastor and the choir singing the first strophe of each hymn, and the congregation only joining in at the second. But at least there is no departure from the old Mecklenburg tradition according to which the pastor chants the prayers and the liturgy in front of the altar. I should not like to forego this custom in any circumstances, even if the clergyman does not have a trained voice ; for it is a part of the Lutheran ritual. I have already had enough cause to regret the fact that the closing liturgy, which was formerly much longer, has been shortened in recent years.

*

The most glorious aspect of Gelbensande is, however, the proximity of the magnificent forest and of the Baltic Sea, which lies like a gleaming sheet of blue, and then again comes raging wildly in. My father bought a spacious and pretty little wooden house at an exhibition in Rostock, and had it put up for my mother as a tea-house in the wood. At first we used to make our excursions to this spot, but it soon became apparent that the position of the little house made it unsuitable for this purpose. It was therefore taken away and put up again on the ridge of a sandhill between Müritz and Graal, where there was a wonderful view of the sea. This solution was a very happy one for us children, and after that we drove there almost every day when the weather was fine.

In the course of time we also got little paddle-boats which were quite flat, though they were provided with air-chambers to guard against the danger of capsizing. But in spite of these it was necessary to sit very still in them, and considerable skill was required to row or paddle the boats correctly. The boats had to be pushed nose first into the water, and then we would get into them. Two men then held the stern and with a jerk pushed the boat out into deeper water, where one had to use the paddle at once so as not to lose weigh against the waves coming in.

On windy days one had first to pass through fairly heavy breakers ; the spray would be flung up and whoever was in the boat would often be wet to the skin. But when one had got away from the beach paddling was easier. This sport, which at that time was still new, had a peculiar attraction for me. Because of the low position in which one sat in the boat, one felt very much the close proximity of the water, and it gave me a strangely exciting sense of direct union with the sea. The little boat would rise and fall with the waves. One's arms had to work valiantly to make the boat progress ; it was as if one were riding on the sea, which was rolling in to the shore in perpetual motion under the boat.

As a rule we kept our boats near the shore, where the castles built by children on holiday were ranged, with their little pennons fluttering gaily in the wind. In my youth the beach was considerably wider than it now is ; more and more land has been carried away by storms since then. Even the sandhills have been undermined and have collapsed, so that our tea-house has several times had to be set further back. At that time everything was still very primitive, and one had to struggle through deep sand to reach the Graal and Müritz piers. Now one can take a stroll along a fine clinkered beach promenade which has been built along the edge of the sandhills.

When it was too rough to go out in the boats we used to dig in the sand, building castles or fortifications and leading the sea water round them through a canal. Then we jumped on our castle and felt as if we were on an island in the sea. One of our best sports was balancing along the groynes which protected the beach from the sea's assaults. We hopped on them from post to post till we got far out and were in danger from the sea and anxious nurses or governesses called us back. For such adventures I generally wore high Russian boots, with which I could go fairly far into the sea.

In the evening, when the sun was setting, we began the journey home. The drive through the glorious woods steeped in the twilight was such a great delight that it was almost the best part of the outing for me. As a rule

we chose a way home that was different from the way
we had come, and now we would pass the luscious open
glades in the wood where the red deer used to gather in
the cool of the evening. We had then to keep as still as
a mouse in order not to frighten the deer.

From quite a distance there was a reddish-yellow
gleam among the trees when a large herd was grazing
peacefully on the green meadowland. If the wind was
blowing against us the carriage might pass unnoticed.
But if we were coming with the wind behind us, the
older animals would soon raise their heads and eye us
attentively while the young ones would move round to
form a herd ; then the leader would take the head, and
they would all be off quickly into the wood. In the
summer, when the stags were still quite trusting, we
often saw them too at the feeding places. It was always
very picturesque to see the proud antlers rising above
the high thick ferns.

But the impression produced was quite different, almost comic, when we came across wild pigs, and the
savage, bristly creatures trotted off through the bushes
with uncouth grunts and rumps raised high. Sometimes
it was a wild sow with her family of striped little pigs
which dashed away in fright, rustling through the dry
foliage as fast as they could. But when I was still small
I always felt a little uneasy when a wild boar, snort-
ing loudly, appeared among the tall ferns in front of
us.

But apart from this there was always deep silence in
the forest in the evenings. The horses went at a walking

pace, and the only sounds were the groaning or scrunch-ing noise made by the wheels, and now and then the tinkle of the harness as one of the four black horses tossed its head.

*

In former times my grandfather or my mother's brothers used to come from Russia to Gelbensande every year for the hunting season. Those were always specially festive occasions for Mama and for us. Our Mecklenburg uncles too were regular guests for the shooting, especially kind Uncle Paul, who could tell such pleasant stories of times gone by.

Once every year, too, the Head of the foundation of the old Clara Convent in Ribnitz made her appearance. She was a dear old lady in a long black silk dress with the ribbon of her order, and a white veil over her head. Soon afterwards we would return the call, visiting the nuns in the convent ; from time to time we also attended divine service in the old convent chapel.

Mama's birthday, the twenty-eighth of July, was always the culminating point of the summer ; it used always to be celebrated at Gelbensande. Long before the day came we sisters were secretly busy with some pre-sent of our own making with which we could give our mother a surprise. My sister used to do coloured poker-work on leather—in the salon there is still a fireguard which she made—and I would make some little handi-craft object or paint a picture. Frau Bock, the proprie-tress of the well-known flower shop in Berlin, would arrive by the first train, in order herself to unpack and arrange the numerous presents which Mama's friends had ordered from her. The centre decoration was always made of Mama's favourite flowers, sweet peas, which at this time of year were in full bloom ; on the table round it, in the most exquisite nosegays and baskets, were glorious roses and carnations. On these birthdays the dining-room was like a flower show and a wonderful fragrance pervaded all the rooms. In later years Frau Bock supplied us in Berlin with the Cotillon bouquets for our balls.

Among other guests on Mama's birthday there was always Baron von Maltzahn who came from Penzlin ; he was one of her most devoted friends. He always made the long journey by carriage, because the railway was too new-fashioned for him, and this made us children always think of him as a survival from a bygone age. It was also part of the birthday tradition that Frau von Oertzen always presented Mama with a cake of her own baking and a basket with guinea-fowl eggs, lying on a bed of salt.

The whole day long telegrams kept pouring in, and we helped Mama as much as we could in answering them. In the afternoon we drove either to the tea-house or to the sea, where the children of the Friedrich–Franz Hospice in Müritz would come to offer their congratulations, or else we played tennis with the guests from Heiligendamm. The lovely day always passed far too quickly for us, for to us children Mama's birthday was a very special day of rejoicing. We still think of those

days with regret, and since Mama's death we still celebrate her birthday quietly every year.

My mother was an enthusiastic tennis player. She
therefore had a court made near the hunting-box and
often invited famous tennis players to stay with us. The
brothers Doherty, for example, stayed with us several
times, and had many hard-fought games with Mama
and her chamberlain, Count Voss, as well as Countess
Clara Schulenburg. Burke, the famous professional,
father of the two well-known brothers, came to Gelbensande regularly every summer for a few weeks, and
practised a great deal with Mama besides giving us
children lessons.

My birthday too was regularly celebrated at Gelbensande. The table of presents always stood in the same
place in the comfortable hall. As my birthday comes
just at the time when heather is in bloom, I was always
given many bunches of heather as a child, and the
memory of these occasions has made it very dear to me.
Early in the morning the Oertzens came to offer their
congratulations ; in the afternoon the children came to
drink chocolate with me, and in the evening all the
servants and grooms assembled, carrying brightly
coloured Chinese lanterns, and marched in a long procession round the lawns in my honour. Gagzow, who
had been our major-domo for many years, headed the
procession. He had come into the Grand-Ducal service
as a footman in Hungarian uniform in grandmama
Marie's time, and had afterwards filled the same post
for my mother, conducting himself so well that she made

him steward of the household both at Cannes and Gelbensande. He was a giant in stature, and the most loyal of all loyal henchmen. When I was a small child he used to carry me in his arms. Little Frau Rust, the housekeeper, who always helped Mama in all household matters, came tripping along beside him. It would take me too far if I tried to enumerate all our old servants and grooms who served us faithfully. I still retain affectionate memories of them all, and think of them as of old friends.

Soon after my birthday Mama used to set off for Paris for her usual autumn visit, and my brother went to Ludwigslust. But I used to stay behind at Gelbensande for a further period, with my governess, Miss King; during this period we lived very cosily quite alone in the shooting-box. We could arrange the whole day just as we liked. Of course lessons took up a great deal of time, but in the time that was left we would make long excursions into the forest, which was every day becoming more autumnal; and we might even stalk the deer which we saw feeding peacefully, often going on all-fours so as to get as close a view of them as possible. Sometimes, too, I would invite my friend Sibylle von Laffert to stay with me for a few days—we had the most glorious games with her—or old Nurse Jenkins would come over from Schwerin. In the evenings after dusk we would walk round near the house, carrying Chinese lanterns and, like all Mecklenburg children, singing the lantern song:

Lantern, Lantern, sun, moon and stars!
Burn up, little candle, burn up bright,
But don't set my beautiful Lantern alight.

Now our daughters walk round with Chinese Lanterns and sing the same dear old song.

Now and then Fräulein von Malschitzki, whom I mentioned before, would come from Schwerin to visit us. Her mother and her aunt had once been governesses to my aunts Marie and Ann. She was a woman of great charm and painted delightful pictures ; she produced many fine water-colours at Gelbensande. We were friends in spite of the difference in age, and until her death a few years ago she was always there to help me with her counsel in many of life's serious problems.

In the evenings after dinner I sometimes played on Mama's grand piano in her beautiful bright salon, or Miss King would entertain me with her piano playing while I could indulge my passion for reading without interruption.

I still like to think of those quiet evenings. I never felt lonely at Gelbensande, even when I was there for weeks alone with my governess. I felt far too closely united with my beloved forest to be lonely. Every rustle of a bird, the faint sighing of the autumn wind in the tree-tops, the falling leaf fluttering through the air, the fleeting tread of deer on soft woodland soil, the snapping of a dead branch or the sharp clash of antlers when a stag fled headlong through the trees, or the sinister bellow of the king of the forest—to me they were all beloved and familiar sounds which filled my soul with gratitude to God and made me feel that I was indissolubly one with the Nature which He had created.

In the evenings before going to sleep I would once more gaze up with a feeling of awe at the tall, thin pines that stood dark and silent about the house, with their branches almost growing in at the windows. All Nature seemed to hold its breath in prayer to its Creator. The peaceful calm of evening touched even my young soul, and I fell asleep, conscious that God was watching over me.

Often I felt impelled to get up very early. At no time is Nature more beautiful than just before sunrise, when the stillness of the forest seems almost audible, while the ground mist lies like a white veil over the fields and the new-born day gradually infuses it with light, until the dark tree-stems take colour from the growing day, the grey beeches begin to show a silver gleam and the pines are turned to gold by the first rays of the rising sun. Such a moment brings an impulse to kneel down and pray. The soul soars upwards to the omnipotence of God, who in unfathomable wisdom and goodness has created everything it is given to us to see. A deep calm comes over us, and our hearts are filled with the certainty that we too are provided for in the divine plan of salvation.

Everyone can participate in this plan of salvation if only he will open his soul to it and subordinate his whole being and everything he does to the will of God, putting unconditional trust in Him. Unlimited strength is given to such a person. His faith can move mountains, if he leaves everything to the higher will. The more his faith endures, the more easily can earthly obstacles be overcome. The ascent to the clear mountain-tops will often meet with set-backs, but faint-heartedness and selfishness must be overcome, for these are the two worst enemies which we shall encounter on the way towards the light. But whoever conquers these is no longer vulnerable ; he will go on his way happy and undaunted, for the Kingdom of God is already opened to him here on earth.

Thoughts such as these come over me when I am in my beloved forest of Gelbensande and find leisure for once to cast aside all the weeds that the bustling earth has wound about my heart and soul.

How devout I felt in my childhood, when I heard the whispering of the tree-tops as, touched by a passing breeze, they bent over to each other ! Nothing is left unsaid in the converse which Nature holds with herself !

The forest shone in its many-hued autumnal splendour, with the clear blue sky overhead, and everything was gleaming and sparkling in the bright sunlight. Gossamer floated like flaxen threads through the air, and settled on dying ferns. Here and there the red of a mountain-ash shone like a torch, and rare pungent smells made one walk faster. I could smell winter. For me, who every year had to fly south like a migrant bird, this premonition of winter had something mysterious in it, something for which I yearned.

Autumn meant death for so much of the beauty that had flowered and grown fairer all through the summer.

For me it meant separation from the northern home I loved ; a gentle melancholy passed over my soul. But for all that I used to get, and I still always get, special strength from these autumn days, from this bitter atmosphere of parting. The dreams of summer with its flowers and its peaceful blue waters draws to an end, and now creative work must be begun.

There, in the Gelbensande forest, into whose peaceful quiet even as a child I took my hopes and my fears, my desires and my supplications to God, there I find refuge even to-day. Thither I make my way, as a pilgrim from a far country goes to the peaceful spring of the hermitage, or as a child flees to his mother's breast.

CHAPTER IV

THE RIVIERA

During my early years we spent many winters on the shores of the blue Mediterranean. But when I speak of our life in Cannes, I must at once admit that, in spite of all the beauty of the southern landscape and its glorious climate, I never got over my longing for our northern home, to which I had to say good-bye every autumn for six months. In the spring I was always impatiently counting the days which had still to pass before we would leave for Mecklenburg. Yet, later on, after I was married, when it seemed as if spring would never come in Berlin or Potsdam, I often felt the call of the Côte d'Azur, with which so many memories of my childhood are associated. Even now I often feel a longing for the beautiful Riviera, and it gives me great pleasure to know that, through all the long years and the war, the people there have not forgotten the " Princesse Cécile " who grew up among them.

We generally arrived in Cannes at the beginning of December, travelling through Lyons and Marseilles or from Paris. From Marseilles on, the journey became extraordinarily beautiful : rich fields of red earth with vines and oak groves across the plain, and in the spring countless almond trees in flower against these red fields—an enchanting vision ! The little trees, delicate and

73

dainty, looked like pink ballet-dancers against the background of heavy clay soil.

Beyond St. Raphael the line ran along close to the shore. The train dashed past red rocks, rising precipitously from the sea, through tunnels, which for several minutes cut off the glorious view; picturesque villages and pine trees spreading like great umbrellas flew past us. In some places the line ran so close to the shore that it seemed as if the white spray of the incoming waves must break over the train. When we had passed the Esterel mountains the bay of La Bocca lay in front of us at last, with the wide valley of the Siagne on the left. I often go back there in memory, recalling beautiful drives and the exquisite flowers I have so often gathered there in the spring. The familiar hotels came into view, the Route de Fréjus, one last tunnel, and then the train slackened speed and drew up panting in the narrow station of Cannes.

Cannes with its green slopes, its wonderful gardens, its white villas and the picturesque Old Town overlooking the harbour, nestles in indescribable beauty on the Côte d'Azur, which nature has so richly endowed. Perhaps Monte Carlo, lying against grey rocks high above the blue Mediterranean, offers a more sublime prospect; Nice with its fine boulevards and shops may be more magnificent—but neither can equal the tranquillity of Cannes, lulled by the murmur of the sea. In the time of my childhood it was still a quiet place, visited only by aristocratic families who led a retired life in their beautiful villas or in the hotels which often almost gave the impression of being their own castles. The noisy social whirl found its place in Nice and Monte Carlo. Since the war it must all be quite different ; Cannes too has grown " mundane " and has acquired a Casino and other noisy places of entertainment. Up to the time of my marriage in the year 1905 there was as yet nothing of that kind.

From the station we drove through the town—in the early years in a carriage, later on in a motor—or more often along by the railway out on to the Route d'Antibes. Then up the steep hill to our own " Villa Wenden " which lay, cheerful and inviting, on the mountain-side.

" Villa Wenden," named after the race from which our family sprang, was a graceful white building in the southern style, facing across gardens and parks right out to the Mediterranean ; my father had had it built in the years 1887 to 1889.

The rooms, nearly all decorated in white, were high and spacious. Only the hall, where we often sat in the evening by the lighted stove, seemed dark and yet very comfortable. The beautiful portrait of my mother, painted by Herkomer in London, used to hang there. All the windows of the great salon faced the sea. Next to the salon was the smoking-room, a sort of winter-garden, entirely fitted with sliding glass sides which could be opened. Here we generally had tea in the after-noon. In the spring the glass doors opening on to the marble steps stood open, and the eye could range far out over the blue Mediterranean, where distant steamers passed on their voyages, or the gaily-coloured sails of the sand-lighters, called " Lesteurs," glided by. On the right the lower ranges of the Esterel mountains were outlined against the western sky, stretching in wonderful contours far out into the sea.

Mama had a delightful balcony, opening out of her boudoir, with a wrought iron railing covered with Maréchal-Niel roses. Glorious wisterias grew on the terrace in front of the smoking-room, and one wall of the house was completely covered with bougainvilleas. Roses flowered almost the whole winter, from November onwards. I too had a lovely balcony, from which I could enjoy the wonderful view of the sea and the Esterels. Very often, in the early morning, just before summer, a Fata Morgana seemed to appear above the horizon to the east : it was the high peaks of the island of Corsica saluting us across the water.

The garden of the villa was in two parts, lying on different levels ; the road between them was crossed by an arched bridge. There were groups of palm trees in the upper garden with its smooth lawns, and the red and yellow fruit of orange and lemon trees glowed among their dark foliage. My favourite place was a pergola completely hidden behind evergreen plants. The garden was shut off from the road below by a high wall, from which wonderful climbing roses hung in trailing wreaths ; looking over it, one seemed to be standing high up on the wall of a fortress.

The narrow bridge connected this " tame " garden with the " wild " garden, as we called the lower slope, where pines and bushes ran riot. A magnificent mimosa

tree flowered here in indescribable splendour every
February ; its little yellow blossoms shone so dazzlingly
in the sun-flooded landscape that it seemed to be made
of sunshine. Later on in Berlin, when the February sky
was still grey or perhaps sleet was falling, I often found
myself thinking of this tree. Now and then I used to see
mimosa in the flower shops, but what were those poor
sprays, exhausted by their long journey, compared with
our tree in the garden of the Villa Wenden ? They say
that it died of cold last winter. Our house has passed
into other hands now—perhaps our mimosa did not
want to serve any other master !

What marvellous sunsets I have seen there ! At first
the sky would be illuminated with every colour of the
rainbow, from deep violet and blood-red to the palest
ethereal green. Gradually the colours grew fainter and
changed to a delicate pink, the Esterels sank into black
shadows, and the evening star rose glittering, until at
last the moon would bathe the gently-moving surface of
the sea in a stream of gold. The accompaniment of this
nocturne was a chorus of frogs, not harsh and croaking
like the toads we know, but like a clear-toned orchestra
of delicate instruments. Thousands of little tree-frogs
sang their serenades in this fashion.

The most beautiful time in Cannes was the end of
April and the beginning of May. The air was mild and
drenched with the sun, now moving from day to day
in almost unbroken ascent on the rising curve of its
course, and bathing everything with light and warmth.
Over the stone walls which shut in the road behind

"Villa Wenden" tiny delicately-scented Banksia roses
fell in white and yellow cascades, and climbed high up
into the palm trees. At midday a gentle breeze ruffled
the surface of the sea. The water lapped softly and
dreamily against the white rocks of the islands. You
could see the bottom of the little bays, and distinguish
every stone and every mussel-shell. The colour of
the water when it was still was a deep glittering
green.

How delightful it was to cross over to the near islands
of St. Marguerite and St. Honorat in those indescribably
beautiful spring days. The return in the late afternoon
was as peaceful as the voyage out in the early morning.
Only the colours of sea and sky had changed. Now we
moved through waves tinged with pink, reflecting the
evening sky, the Esterels lay in deep purple shadow on
our right, and the colour of the sky faded to a pale
opalescence.

The days were not always so bright, nor was the sky
always blue and cloudless. From time to time a wet
spell would set in, which generally plunged the whole
landscape for three days into impenetrable grey in
which mountains and sea disappeared. Then it rained
day and night. The heavy downpour fell with a
monotonous rhythm and mercilessly imprisoned human
beings indoors. But to me these wet days were
often most welcome, because then at least I had
time for reading, which I seldom got on ordinary
school-days.

When at last the rain was over, the southern sun would

shine forth in all its glory, and the deep blue sea and the wonderful Alps, glittering far off with newly-fallen snow, became once more visible in an almost blinding wealth of colour.

But when the " Mistral," the west wind, sprang up the landscape changed much more rapidly. In the early morning the sea would be quite calm and smooth ; only the mountains seemed to draw nearer and nearer, and the most distant trees and rocks could be clearly distinguished. Gradually the sky took on a deep blue tinge, and light clouds blew up, fluttering in the wind like little flags. Towards midday the bay would be covered with white breakers, the wind freshened, and soon the mistral, increasing rapidly in strength towards the evening, would be raging over sea and land. In the night it became almost a hurricane. It bent the palms like wisps of fluff whirled hither and thither by a giant, it howled with deafening noise round the corners of the house, and shook the walls so that it almost seemed as if the house would collapse. But I loved it, and felt at home in the unfettered elements.

Many years later, when we were living in the " seahouse " at Zoppot, I experienced similar storms, coming from the north. But they seldom had the giant force, the exulting triumphant strength with which the mistral raged across the land.

How grateful I am to fate for those early impressions, and for the privilege of having grown up amid such glorious surroundings ! In my mind's eye I can still see the marvels of Nature in the south and indeed I can say that the southern landscape has become one of my spiritual possessions.

*

In this earthly paradise my parents could follow their inclinations without hindrance, and above all could devote themselves to sport and social intercourse.

In those days my parents' enthusiasm for open-air activities was still something rather uncommon. As I have already mentioned, my mother was a keen tennis-player. She took part, either as a player or as a spectator, in every tennis tournament that was held on the courts of the Hotel Beau-Site in Cannes. Many international tennis stars used to play in Cannes, including the veteran lawn-tennis champion, Mr. Simpson. My mother's chamberlain, Count Voss, for many years a leading German player, successfully upheld the honour of Germany on the tennis-courts.

My father devoted himself, as far as his health allowed, to sailing, in which he took great pleasure. For several years he owned the sailing-yacht *Aranella*, which was replaced later on by the touring-yacht *Palatina*. He was a winner at many regattas in which he competed with English and French yachts in the Bay of Cannes and La Bocca. The trophies still adorn the fine hall of the shooting-box at Gelbensande. We three children inherited our love of the sea and our passion for sailing from my father, and to our delight these have been transmitted to our own children. In fact, nothing gave me greater pleasure than to be on the water. How often

we made the trip to St. Honorat and St. Marguerite in
our brown steam-launch *Fée*, breakfasted there in some
lovely spot under the fragrant pines, and then set out on
an expedition through the woods or a break-neck climb
on the white rocks ! It frequently happened that the
French fleet would be lying at anchor in the " Golfe de
Juan." On those occasions it was interesting to make it
the aim of our trip to steam round these colossal black
giants. How often in those days we passed peacefully
right through the French fleet, with the German naval
ensign at our stern, little thinking that this fleet would
one day be our enemy.

I enjoyed it particularly when the sea was rough and
our bows plunged deep into the oncoming waves while
the screw astern raced in the air, with a loud pounding
noise. Ever and again the buoyant launch would rise
victorious and scale the mountainous waves. It was
glorious and at the same time rather terrifying. But my
escort could not acquire any taste at all for this pitching
movement, and so when the sea was rough we had to
keep close in shore, where, however, the ground-swell
generally gave us a fairly rough passage, or else we made
for sheltered waters. As a rule I had to take my books
with me, to prepare my lessons, but probably nothing
much came of it—surrounded as we were by the over-
mastering beauty of nature, which filled me with endless
admiration !

I remember one expedition to the island of St. Marguerite, which I made with two girl friends in a little
open sailing boat, that nearly came to a tragic end. We

had set out in the morning in the most beautiful weather, with a light wind. But when we were having breakfast in the glorious pine wood on the south side of the island, a strong breeze sprang up and in a short time became a regular storm. The captain, who was anxious about the return voyage, steered the boat round the point of the island and took us up the north side facing the mainland, quite close to the fortress where once the historic " Iron Mask " was kept prisoner for many years. From there the crossing to the " Pointe de la Croisette," the nearest landing-place, was only a few miles wide.

We were hardly out of the shelter of the island when the wind caught our little sailing boat and tossed it hither and thither, so that our brave sailors began to pull very long faces. The waves had risen considerably within a few hours, and every now and then they broke over our low gunwale, filling the boat with water and by degrees soaking us all to the skin. It was a very unpleasant situation, and I remember that we three young girls and our escort suffered no little anxiety as to whether we should ever reach the land in safety.

At any rate we were heartily glad when at last we felt firm ground under our feet once more. This little incident destroyed my taste for the sea for a long time, and I was thoroughly nervous whenever the *Fée* ran into a heavy sea. But by degrees this nervousness disappeared and I recovered my great delight in boating.

Every year we made fairly long sea-trips as the guests of an American lady, Mrs. Robert Goelet, on her beautiful white steam-yacht *Nahma*. Mrs. Goelet was a most charming lady, who had suffered much from ill-health and the repeated blows of fate, and sought consolation and health at sea in her exquisite floating home. She had lost her only daughter, who was of my own age, soon after one of our joint expeditions to the islands, and I think she was so fond of me personally because I somehow reminded her of her dead daughter. Later on Mrs. Goelet often came for the Kiel regatta, and received the distinction of a visit from my father-in-law. At that time I was once more her guest on a beautiful voyage from Travemünde to Danzig, but she was then already very ill and could hardly walk. Six months later her sufferings found an end. Mrs. Goelet and her *Nahma* belong to the dearest memories of my youth. I remember with profound gratitude the feasts of beauty which this kindly American lady enabled me to enjoy.

One experience belonging to a rather later period, the memory of which is closely associated with Cannes, may be added here. This was a voyage we made in the year 1903 on the Russian battleship *Rjetwjesan* which was then on her way to the Far East. (The name is of Norman origin and is derived from the words Recht-wis-an.) My mother and I travelled to Toulon, where we went on board the great warship, which was of the most modern type then known. It was a gloriously sunny day, and the voyage was extremely enjoyable. The view of the Riviera coast from the sea was superb : in the foreground the low wooded hills, and beyond the Maritime Alps clothed in snow. But I could not escape from the

thought that this ship and these men were now on their
way to the Far East, to far distant places, separated from
their homes by half the world.

We had already been in Toulon several times before,
when a Russian battleship was being built there. The
commandant and some of his officers, who were super-
intending its completion, lived with their families in the
neighbourhood of Toulon. We spent many happy hours
in those beautiful surroundings with the commandant,
Grigorovich, who later on became Naval Minister, and
his wife and daughter.

*

For me the chief charm of the holidays lay in the fact
that they meant my brother's arrival in Cannes. Mlle.
Pascon, one of my governesses, always asserted with a
smile that when I said to her " mon frère arrive " my
eyes used to light up, a sign that I was expecting something specially delightful. That was indeed the case, and
it is just the same to this day, whenever I am looking
forward to a meeting with my brother.

When my brother came of age in the year 1901, he
took over the government of his country. The consciousness of being called to such a responsible post at the age
of nineteen made him mature beyond his years and gave
him a serious outlook on life. According to family tradition he also became my guardian, and perhaps this
circumstance gave my relation to him, which had always
been very close, a still greater intimacy.

How glorious it was to be able to go in for all sorts of

things with him in those days in Cannes ! At such times
my mother would relax the strict rule that I must always
have an escort, and entrusted me to the sole care of my
brother. In the mornings we used often to walk down
into the town, or to the harbour, which was always full
of interest for us, and we established records in the time
we took to get there. As my brother generally brought
his motor, we were able to make the most beautiful
excursions into the surrounding country. The roads
almost everywhere were in splendid condition, and it
was wonderful to drive up the hills and past quaint old
mountain towns, with glorious views of the sea and the
olive-covered slopes. On one occasion my brother gave
me sole control of his car, which came some time before
his own arrival, and this made me feel particularly
proud.

*

I have already said that my parents were very fond of
society, although they had no taste for formal court
functions. As a rule it was a small circle that gathered
round them, at mid-day or in the evening. My parents
always received their guests, whether of high rank or
low, with the same hospitality and simplicity. For this
reason they were beloved by everybody, and everyone
felt at home with them. My parents also maintained a
lively social intercourse with foreign royalties and interesting personages who came to the Riviera. I used often
to be called down to greet them ; and the recollection
of them is impressed more or less vividly on my memory.

Above all I remember with perfect clearness the Prince of Wales, afterwards King Edward VII ; he was one of the regular visitors to Cannes, and he was greatly beloved among all sections of the people. His uncle, the Duke of Cambridge, and his sons were also among the regular visitors. Queen Victoria too liked to visit the Riviera, but she preferred Nice, where she stayed at the Regina Palace Hotel. Once when I was ten years old my mother took me to lunch there in order to present me to her. I can still see the old lady, very small and bent, as she received us in her wheeled chair. Behind her stood two strapping Indians, who also waited on her at table. Her daughters, the Princess Helena and Beatrice, were there too, but these two estimable ladies had little to say in the presence of their royal mother. An atmosphere of formality and constraint has never appealed to me, and I must admit that I found this visit rather uncongenial. Of course at the time I knew nothing of Queen Victoria's historical importance. From time to time we also visited the Duchess of Edinburgh and her four beautiful and talented daughters in Nice ; their charming water-colour paintings aroused my whole-hearted admiration and my secret envy, because I used to make some attempts in this direction myself.

I have a very delightful recollection of a meeting, which took place when I was nearly grown-up, with the Empress Eugenie, widow of Napoleon III. The old lady came to Cannes to visit my mother ; her faithful secretary Pétri and an elderly lady-in-waiting were among her suite. My mother instructed us beforehand that we

must be very polite to the Empress, call her "Your
Majesty" as a matter of course, and treat her with the
greatest respect; just because she had been deposed it
was necessary to make it easier for her by continuing to
use the form of address to which she was accustomed.
We found the Empress most charming and unaffected.
Unmistakable traces of her once famous beauty were
still visible in her face with its regular features and vivid
eyes. Her mind was as clear as ever, her memory amaz-
ing and her conversation full of vivacity. Her personality, historically and individually so compelling, made
a lasting impression on me.

At our parents' villa too we often saw three ladies who
had been the intimate friends of the Empress Eugenie
when the Second Empire was at its zenith : the Marquise
de Gallifet, widow of the general who was renowned
for his foolhardy cavalry attack at Sedan on September 1,
1870, Countess Melanie Pourtalès and Princess Sagan.
They were highly accomplished in the art of conversation, and could talk fascinatingly of the Empress, the
Emperor and their son, the unfortunate Prince Loulou,
who was killed as a volunteer in the Zulu war. The
delightful General Charette, whose Louis Napoleon
beard recalled the great days of the past even in externals,
was often to be found in the society of these three ladies ;
he had been our grandfather's chivalrous enemy in the
great winter campaign on the Loire.

After I was engaged my mother and I once again
visited the Empress Eugenie at Cap Martin, when she
received us in her beautiful Villa Cyrnos. This visit from

me, as the betrothed of the Crown Prince of Germany, evidently gave her great pleasure, and in the course of conversation she questioned me most eagerly about the Crown Prince. After that, unfortunately, I never met the Empress Eugenie again, although she only died a few years ago.

My Russian uncles were in the habit of visiting us one after the other in the course of the winter, and my grandfather also came regularly to Cannes, but he used to stay at one of the hotels. For me those were always delightful times, full of variety. I used to play piano duets with my aunt, the Grand Duchess Georg, and this generally led to great mutual hilarity, because my fingers would not always keep up, and I had to resort to invention so as to keep in time. In particular Grieg's *Death of Asa* always reduced us to peals of laughter instead of producing the proper solemnity. In my young days I suffered from an irresistible inclination to laugh at the most inappropriate times. However satisfactory a good laugh may be at suitable moments, it can be torture in situations where obvious mirth is not at all the right thing.

I always looked forward with special pleasure to the visit of the Grand Duke Nikolai, my mother's eldest brother. He was the only one of my uncles who took me seriously and never teased me, and to a sensitive child or schoolgirl that means a great deal ! With his tall figure, his broad shoulders and his high forehead, Uncle Nikolai gave an impression of great mental superiority. He was a keen student of history, much taken up with historical researches, and an ardent collector and connoisseur of historical miniatures. He had published a number of historical works. The University of Berlin had given him an honorary doctor's degree, and he had been elected a member of the Institut de France. He could talk entrancingly of his studies, and made me keenly interested in history in general and family history in particular. He was a firm believer in the royal descent of Kaspar Hauser and had written an unpublished book on the subject. He had probably had access to the archives, through his close relationship to the house of Baden.

Uncle Nikolai was very fond of the Casino at Monte Carlo, and was always very lucky; but he possessed the rare and valuable gift of being able to stop at the right moment. When he had won a fair amount he was very generous and would bring back for my mother or for me some exquisite piece of jewellery from the wonderful jewellers' shops in Monte Carlo or Nice. On one occasion he made a present of a motor to one of his near relations, because he thought that she had brought him luck at the tables.

Because of his magnanimous and sympathetic character, he was extraordinarily beloved by his friends. But he could be very sarcastic with outsiders and people who disagreed with him. He had a bitter and unsparing tongue for anyone he disliked. But to people whom he was fond of and found congenial he remained a loyal and affectionate friend. In my childhood and later on in my early married life I took a special pride in being on good terms with this revered uncle. He too was a victim of the Bolshevist murderers.

Sometimes we used to lunch with acquaintances, including the family of Lord Brougham, whose father had been one of the founders of Cannes. The Château Eléonore with its magnificent park was a real beauty spot and we spent many pleasant hours as the guests of this hospitable man ; his daughter was one of my early friends, and I kept up with her for years afterwards. A small circle of my mother's close friends generally gathered there, as well as at the house of Mrs. Winslow, an American friend of my mother's. She was the owner of a steam yacht, on which we often made joint trips to the islands. In the evening we generally had guests at our villa. After dinner they used to play poker with my mother and my brother.

Whenever visitors were expected my mother would send me early in the morning with my governess to the flower market to get flowers to decorate the table, and for me these commissions were both an honour and a delight. We used to go from stall to stall, buying violets, tulips or some other flowers. The masses of carnations, wallflowers, tulips and many others, piled up on separate stalls or standing in pails, were a wonderful feast of colour. We had our favourite market women, from whom we liked best to make our purchases ; and they kept a sharp look-out to see that we did not buy too much from their neighbours. We used to drive home laden with our fragrant purchases. In the evening the dining-table was adorned with our trophies, and we had the proud sense of having contributed materially to its decoration.

*

During our residence in Cannes my parents always had an escort of one lady-in-waiting and one or two gentlemen, although strictly speaking there was no " court." But their relations were those of friends rather than of servants. I have already said that the Lord High Steward and his wife, the Count and Countess Alexander Bassewitz, used to remain in Mecklenburg as deputies for my parents ; now and then they came on a short visit to Cannes. Secretary of State von Bülow used to come very often, on the other hand, in order to transact State business with my father. When Countess Bassewitz retired on account of her health she was succeeded by Baroness von Maltzahn, wife of General Fritz von Maltzahn, who for many years was my father's Adjutant-General. The General was head of the military department of the Mecklenburg section of the army, which included the 89th Grenadier Regiment in Schwerin, the 90th Fusiliers in Rostock and Wismar, two regiments of Dragoons, the 17th in Ludwigslust and the 18th in Parchim, as well as the 60th Artillery Regiment in Schwerin and the 14th Rifle Battalion in Colmer (Alsace). The von Maltzahns were among the most intimate friends of my parents. The general, an aristocratic and intelligent man, was my father's counsellor not only on military questions but in everyday affairs. His wife endeared herself to us all by her gaiety and friendliness, and their sons were our playmates.

The general remained in office after my father's death, both during the regency of my Uncle Johann Albrecht, and during my brother's reign, until death deprived us of his counsel. After my brother's marriage the Baroness became deputy Mistress of the Robes to my sister-in-law Alexandra. In her place my mother appointed Frau von der Schulenburg to the office of Lady-in-Waiting when a long journey or a court function required that a lady should be in attendance. Frau von Schulenburg often spent months with us in Cannes.

We were all specially attached, as far as I remember, to Count Wilhelm Schwanenfeld-Schwerin, among my father's adjutants, because of his chivalrous character. He used to call me " Sunshine " and was always kindness itself to me as a little girl. He left us a short time before Papa's death, but as long as he lived he remained our faithful friend. I saw him again not long before his death, when he was very ill in a sanatorium in Berlin. It was a most affectionate and touching re-union ; he had kept his kindly interest in my brother and sister and myself through all those years. Count Schwerin's successor was Herr von Kap-Herr of the Potsdam Life-Guards ; he took up his office just before my father's death, and was with us during those sad days in Cannes.

Among my mother's ladies-in-waiting, I was specially fond of Fräulein von Suckow, because she was always willing to play with me, and was never tired of telling me about my dear great-grandmother, to whom she had previously been lady-in-waiting. She left us to go to Grandmama Marie, and, with her colleague the Baroness von Stenglin, remained in her service as one of her ladies-in-waiting until Grandmama's death in 1922.

After Fräulein von Suckow, Baroness Luise of Maltzan of the House of Wartenberg and Penzlin, became lady-in-waiting to my mother ; she was a gifted and helpful companion and showed the utmost devotion and loyalty to my mother. When she married her cousin, who was Marshal of the Court at Neustrelitz, Fräulein von Lefort came to be with my mother, but she stayed only a few years because she too soon married.

Count Victor Voss must be mentioned first among my mother's chamberlains; he was her escort for many years when she travelled and in all sporting events. I have already spoken of his distinction as a tennis-player. He was also a brilliant shot and a great lover of horses. In the year 1897 he learnt to drive a car, and thus was probably one of the earliest amateur drivers in Germany. It was particularly pleasant and appropriate for my parents to have a keen sportsman as a member of their suite, because of their own interest in sport.

When Count Voss resigned he was followed by Herr von Gordon, who was also an accomplished tennis-player, and Count Bassewitz-Prebberede who was my mother's escort on several journeys to Russia and was also present at my wedding as her official chamberlain. My mother, like every Russian Grand Duchess, also had a Russian secretary who looked after her business affairs.

When I recall to my mind these figures from my

93

parents' entourage, I think I may say that, as the result of a wise selection, they were never the agents of intrigue, perhaps the most hideous monster that can appear in any Court. Indeed it is my opinion that royal families are themselves chiefly responsible for it, if they endure around them people who cherish envy and ill-will towards each other.

*

My most vivid memories of my father are associated with Christmas in Cannes. About four o'clock on Christmas Eve he always drove down with us three children in a closed landau to the German church. There a Christmas tree would already be lighted up, and its brilliance filled us with the most delightful anticipations.

Our excitement at the thought of the presents waiting for us at home probably prevented us from being very attentive during the sermon, but the Christmas carols and the solemn atmosphere filled our hearts with a sense of profound reverence. When we came out of the church the twilight of Christmas Eve had already fallen. The drive back and the steep climb up to our villa made severe demands on our patience. My father generally lighted a cigarette on the way, using a wax-match for the purpose ; and to this day the smell of a lighted wax-match reminds me of those Christmas drives.

At home there was generally a new dress, with the silk shoes belonging to it, lying ready for me. Then we had to dress very quickly, our hearts beating with excitement, and afterwards we went down into the large salon, where the whole household was assembled in front of the closed doors of the hall. The suspense reached its climax. At last my father would ring a bell, and instantly the doors were opened, as if by unseen hands ; and we stood dazzled in front of the giant Christmas tree, and the tables loaded with wonderful presents.

Exquisite sweets in all sorts of shapes hung on the tree ; I particularly remember one that was made to look like a white muff. I was always very fond of fur, and this miniature imitation delighted me. The branches were festooned with long chains of bright-coloured sugar balls, and fat marzipan sausages and other decorations hung on ribbons in the Mecklenburg colours. These decorations were always ordered from Krefft's, the confectioners in Schwerin. A hugh marzipan cake, made to resemble the castle at Schwerin, always stood underneath the tree. This was to remind us of our beloved and far-distant home.

On Christmas morning my mother used to drive with us to the evangelical church, a custom which she kept up until the time of my marriage. In return we used often to go with her to the Russian church on Russian festivals.

After my father's death my mother could not make up her mind to celebrate Christmas Eve at the Villa Wenden. So we used to spend it with my uncle the Grand Duke Michail and his wife, Countess Sophie Torby (née Countess Merenberg), and their family at

their elegant Villa Kasbek. For me it was always infinitely distressing to have to be away from home just at
Christmas ; I had always been so delighted to go down
early in the morning on Christmas Day into the room
where the Christmas tree stood, and I missed this most
of all. But my small cousins were such dear little girls,
and my uncle and aunt were so kind to us, that Christmas Eve was generally very pleasant all the same. It
was only two years before my marriage that Mama con-
sented to stay at home in the Villa Wenden for the
present-giving, but we did not have it in the hall, as in
Papa's lifetime, because that would have been too distressing for her.

How my mother used to spoil me ! I nearly always
had some beautiful piece of furniture or work of art, and
invariably some good books. In the course of time I
received in this way as presents nearly all our German
classics as well as the works of French and English poets,
and later on, when I had made some progress in my
knowledge of the Russian language, the works of Russian
poets too. It was thus that the foundations of my own
little library were laid ; I have always tried to go on
adding to it, and it has become one of my most precious
possessions.

We children frequently took part with our mother in
the observance of the Russian festivals which were celebrated by the numerous Russian residents in Cannes.
In this connection I remember specially the Easter
celebrations which took place at midnight in the pretty
Russian church. Beforehand I had to lie down in bed,

so as to be prepared for the midnight ceremony. We used to drive down to the church, all of us dressed in white according to the Russian custom, a little before midnight. The congregation walked in procession three times round the church, each carrying a lighted candle, led by the priests and the choir chanting hymns. Then the doors were opened and we entered the brilliantly-lighted church to join in the solemn service. Exactly at twelve o'clock the church-bells, which had been silent all through Lent, rang out, clear and joyful. The priest cried "Christ is risen!" and the congregation responded, " He is truly risen ! " and everyone present, particularly those who were related to one another, embraced and kissed each other three times.

There was a wonderful Easter-feast at home afterwards, with the most exquisite Russian dishes, and all kinds of pastry. The strictly orthodox had fasted for six weeks, so the appetite with which these dainties were devoured may well be imagined ! There was a kind of sweet cream served in the shape of a pyramid decorated with a paschal lamb and palm-branches and eaten with rich raisin cake, which I always found particularly tasty.

*

An important event in the course of the winter of 1896–7 was our making the acquaintance of the family of the Duke of Cumberland, who had taken up his residence at the Park Hotel in Cannes for the sake of the health of his eldest son Georg Wilhelm. The Duke of

Cumberland was one of the noblest men I have ever known : always kindly and sympathetic, of sterling character, honourable and loyal to everyone, even towards those who might be his political enemies. The family had early become acquainted with sorrow, and for this reason there was a spirit of sympathy and unselfishness in the relations between parents and children which is not often to be met with.

The three daughters, Marie-Louise, afterwards Princess Max of Baden, my future sister-in-law Alexandrine, and Olga were of about the same age as my sister and I, and we very soon became firm friends ; Olga and I, in spite of the two years' difference in age, were as much devoted to each other, after a time, as twins. The younger sons Christian and Ernst August, afterwards Duke of Braunschweig, were our merry playmates, and we took great delight in the society of the Cumberland children. They often came to tea with us, or else we used to make joint excursions.

My father's health grew worse from month to month in the course of this winter. Unfortunately I do not remember that period very clearly. He was very ill, and as a result lived in great seclusion, so that I was not often allowed to see him. In March 1897 he and my mother, who was untiring in her care of him, moved to the little town of Grasse, which lies above Cannes, and is famous for its perfumeries. The change of air actually did give him some relief.

In March Prince Christian, the present King of Denmark, came to Cannes, and on a certain memorable

day—March 22, the centenary of the birth of the old
Emperor—we went on a fairly long excursion to St.
Marguerite. In the course of this expedition my sister
became engaged to Prince Christian. He immediately
set out for Grasse, in order to ask for my parents' blessing. I only heard of this event on the following day, and
I remember that at first the news reduced me to bitter
tears, because the thought of losing my sister seemed
quite unbearable. Adini, as she is called in the family,
had always been the centre of the household, her sunny
nature radiating harmony and balance. She was unselfishness personified. She never wanted things for
herself, never pushed herself forward, and always tried
to give happiness to others, even at the expense of her
own wishes. To me, her little sister, she was always like
that : she was my best friend. I can record our intimate
sisterly affection with a thankful heart as one of the
precious gifts of my life. My grief at the prospect of
separation was therefore justified. But my brother-
in-law soon succeeded not only in comforting me,
but in winning my affection and friendship by his
kindness, and since then we have become the best of
friends.

My sister's engagement was a great joy to my father ;
it was to be his last. At the beginning of April he returned
to Cannes. On the morning of the 10th I saw my beloved
father for the last time ; he was sitting in a wheeled
chair in my mother's large salon, and he looked very
ill and weak, but he was as kind as ever. In the evening
when we were at dinner with our companions one after

another was summoned, but I was left up there. I realised that something very sad was happening.

About nine o'clock our old English physician and friend Dr. Blanc came to me, put his hand on my head and said with great emotion : " It is a very sad thing to lose one's father." Then suddenly I realised with terrible clearness that I no longer had a father. I can still feel the sense of desolation and the infinite loneliness that overwhelmed me at that moment. How we children missed my dear father all the rest of our lives, and how I have always envied others who were not fatherless !

The next morning my mother took me into the chamber of death. Papa lay in bed with folded hands, looking peaceful and beautiful, as if he were asleep, so that I had none of that terrifying sense of death, but only a feeling of profound solemnity.

The following days were agitated and full of events. Various relations came hurriedly from Germany. My brother had arrived just the day before my father's death, so that he had been able to be with him at the last. In the evening a short service was held beside my father's open coffin, which lay in his writing-room. There was such a profusion of flowers that the wreaths covered the long landing in front of my parents' rooms, and the heavy scent of these slowly-fading flowers filled the whole stairway. For years the peculiar scent of wall-flowers reminded me of that sad time.

On the evening before the removal of the body to Ludwigslust there was a memorial service, attended by many of our relations and friends in Cannes. When the strangers had gone my mother and we children took leave of our father and kissed his hand for the last time.

The next day there was a parade of French troops in front of the railway station, the French Republic honouring in this way a German ruling prince. The railway coach, draped in black, which carried my father's body home to Mecklenburg, started immediately and my mother followed with my brother and sister. They did not take me with them; they wanted to spare me, because of my youth, the fatigue and all the sad impressions of that journey.

As my brother, the heir to the throne, was not of age at the time of my father's death, my uncle Johann Albrecht acted as Regent for him until his majority in the year 1901. In those few years of the Regency my uncle's strong sense of reverence for my father led him to act in complete accordance with my father's wishes, and he was able to carry out what his brother had begun but had never been able to complete. His keen sense of duty, the outcome of deep religious feeling, brought the country great benefits. The years of his work have never been forgotten in Mecklenburg.

While my family went home for the funeral ceremony I went with my governess to the Duke and Duchess of Cumberland at the Park Hotel, where I was received like a child of the house. Parents and children, as well as their grandmother, the Queen of Hanover, did everything they could to help me through those painful days until the return of my mother and sister. My great affection and unbounded respect for this beloved family date from that time, when they looked after me with so much kindness.

At the end of April my mother and Adini came back and we stayed on at Cannes longer than usual, until well into May. Filled with sadness my sister and I once again sailed on my father's yacht, taking our deep sorrow out to the open sea. She was soon, alas, to be ours no more. But we kept the trim brown steam-launch *Fée*, which had always accompanied my father when he went sailing.

*

We did not spend the summer of 1897 in Schwerin, because it would have been too painful for my mother to be there without my father. I remained at Gelben-sande, while my mother travelled to Denmark with my sister, in order to present her to the royal family as the future bride of Prince Christian. My sister was received with great cordiality by King Christian IX and Queen Louise and the whole family, so that she soon felt quite at home.

Then my mother and Adini went to Russia. After their return my future brother-in-law Christian visited us at Gelbensande, and won all our hearts by his gaiety and friendliness. He used to entertain us delightfully with his amusing stories and his light-hearted ways. I was his best audience, but my noisy mirth used to annoy my sister when we were going through the forest, where she liked to watch the wild creatures. She used to command us to be silent, but without any noticeable effect, as my brother-in-law never stopped making jokes and I could not stop splitting my sides with laughing at them. The innocent charm of those days is unforgettable.

Soon after this a Danish lady, Fröken Bunsen, came to us, to teach my sister the Danish language. She was brilliantly successful, for when the young Princess Christian went to her new home she had an almost complete mastery of the language of the country.

The year 1897 was not to end without inflicting yet another heavy loss upon our family ; the death of Duke Friedrich Wilhelm. My uncle, who was in command of the torpedo boat S26, had just returned to Wilhelmshaven after long autumn manœuvres in the North Sea ; the long white pennant fluttered at the mast. On September 22, on the return voyage of the Duke's torpedo-boat division from Wilhelmshaven to Kiel, not far from the first lightship on the Elbe, an extraordinarily strong following ground-swell caught his boat and caused it to turn turtle. The unlucky vessel floated keel up on the water. The other boats hurried to the rescue as quickly as they could and saved most of the crew. But my uncle, who at the moment of the catastrophe had been standing on the bridge, was swept by the rush of water into the 'tweendecks, where he found five of the men, only one of whom could swim. Recognising the hopelessness of the situation in which he and his men were placed, he uttered a prayer with complete self-control and devotion: " Father, receive our souls into thy keeping and grant us a swift and easy death." Then he ordered the stoker who could swim to save himself, and to make it known that he was in the 'tweendecks. Thus, instead of saving himself as he might have done, being a good swimmer, this heroic man was faithful to his subordinates even unto death, and by this deed showed himself worthy of his ancient lineage. It was only several days later, after the bodies of the sailors had been found, that his body was recovered ; his features had an expression of infinite sternness, but at the same time of absolute tranquillity.

The death of her eldest son was a very heavy blow to Grandmama Marie, and a great loss to us all. We were particularly devoted to Uncle Friedrich Wilhelm because of his happy disposition and his seaman's courage.

We returned to Cannes early in the autumn of this disastrous year. My sister had begged to be allowed to postpone the date of her marriage, so as not to leave my mother so soon after my father's death, but to wait until the year of mourning was over. We daughters wore black for a year, and grey or mauve for another six months. This seems strange nowadays when even for near relations the period of mourning is very short.

We spent that winter very quietly, and only the visits of my future brother-in-law Christian made a break in our retirement. There was one incident, however, which caused great excitement. One Sunday Count Voss proposed that the betrothed pair should go for a motor drive. They drove out, free from any forebodings, to the more distant surroundings of Cannes. On the steep part of one of the mountain roads the car suddenly skidded, struck against the kerb and plunged down the slope. As the speed of cars in those days was not very great,

GRAND DUKE FRIEDRICH FRANZ III AT GELBENSANDE

nothing serious happened to the occupants, and they escaped with the shock and a few bruises. Although I was not personally concerned in it, this incident was a great event in my childhood. The accident completely spoilt my brother-in-law's pleasure in motoring for years to come.

But one person was not to be frightened off by it, and this was my mother. In the very same year she bought a car from the firm of Panhard-Levasseur, in which she took fairly long drives. It attracted a great deal of attention everywhere, because this mode of travelling was still almost unknown. The car itself strikes us nowadays as indescribably comic. The correct form for the technical requirements of the motor-car had not yet been discovered ; actually it looked very much as if a motor had been built on in front of one of the old coaches. But it showed great foresight on my mother's part to accustom herself to motoring in those days. She became patroness of the first German automobile club, afterwards the Imperial Automobile Club, now the Automobile Club of Germany. Connections were established with the Central European Motor Car Union ; a few years before the war the Union, under the leadership of its president, Count Talleyrand-Perigord, organised a pilgrimage to Gelbensande in which a large number of cars took part.

My sister's marriage took place on the twenty-sixth of April, 1898. For me of course this was a very great and decisive event. It meant that my only sister was leaving home, and it involved the breaking up of the happy society of her friends in which I had been allowed to share, although, because I was so much younger, sometimes only on sufferance. Now I was to be altogether alone.

The wedding was celebrated in the presence of many royal relatives on both sides in the unpretentious German church in Cannes. It was raining (which is supposed to bring luck) and my feelings were quite in keeping with the weather. I could not restrain my tears, and infected my sister with my sentimentality. But God has bestowed on these two dear people such profound happiness in life that our wedding tears have been long since forgotten.

CHAPTER V

TRAINING AND EDUCATION

In the early years of my life I was under the care of Miss Mary Jenkins, the English nurse who had already brought up my sister and my brother. Opinions may differ on the custom of placing English nurses in charge of royal nurseries. But it must be remembered that thirty or forty years ago the care given to children among us in Germany was not on as high a level as it was later. I myself deliberately broke with this custom for my children, but it is true only when the traditional English nurse had not been altogether successful with my first child. With the active help of my mother-in-law, Kaiserin Auguste Viktoria, who applied herself with the greatest devotion to this important sphere, our hygienic arrangements and our experience in child-welfare have made rapid progress. I believe it is not an exaggeration for me to say that in this matter we have already surpassed the English.

I consider that it is a mistake to entrust children at their most tender age to a foreigner, who naturally is not in a position to convey elementary ideas to her foster-children in their mother tongue. She must lack familiarity with the children's songs, the dear little rhymes and everything that binds a child to his nation through the spiritual values shared with it. Here too

107

insignificant causes produce great effects ! I must, however, say, on the basis of my own experience, that
although English was my first language I never suffered
any ill-effects from it. A great deal that, as a child, I did
not perhaps pick up as easily as other children of my age,
I managed to get hold of quickly when I was older,
including familiarity with the German language. The
advantages I gained were permanent, that is to say, a
thorough and perfectly natural knowledge of English,
and with it probably also an appreciation of many
English peculiarities, although I have only once been in
England since I was grown up.

In practice this question has now been settled, on the
whole probably in favour of the German method ; what
appears to me of far greater importance is the problem
of the ethical aims of training, because it seems to me
that a regrettable change of attitude towards all values
is gaining ground in this country at the present time. I
feel that there are two conceptions which more than any
others are essential to give real intrinsic worth to a
character which is in process of formation: respect for
the living and reverence for the dead. And these were
the conceptions which our parents instilled in us as the
basic principles in our lives. Respect for everything honourable in humanity was to them a natural attitude of
mind on the part of young people. And no one ever
spoke otherwise than reverently of our dead grandparents, great-grandparents and other relatives. We
never heard an unkind or even disapproving or disparaging remark about other people such as might have

produced in our youthful minds that passion for criticism which threatens to poison the souls of our young people at the present time.

We grew up, therefore, accustomed to respect older people and to show consideration to our fellow human beings. We were in the habit of taking a sincere interest in the life of people who belonged to the past. With what sensitive interest and reverence we used to roam through the rooms of these people who were dead, looking at the things which had been dear to them and were still reverently preserved, and keeping their memory fresh by thus forming a picture of their everyday life. ·

It has often surprised me to find how few people really think historically—not only people of the present day in general, but even members of ruling Houses ! How much they would save themselves and others if they did ! It is not clinging tenaciously to external forms of arrogant conduct that proves descent from personalities who have had historical importance, but—*noblesse oblige !*—making it the guiding principle of one's life, precisely because of the obligations imposed by past history, to act always with a full consciousness of one's duty and an undeviating sense of responsibility to both the present and the future !

It often grieves me, therefore, to have to realise how little interest is taken by the present generation in its progenitors and their fate. This can no doubt be explained by the hurry of modern life, conditioned as it is by the hard struggle to live. For that reason I believe that we, who in our youth were trained in the tradition of respect for the past, must be particularly careful to maintain the sense of reverence in our children.

What insight and understanding Mama showed in guiding every aspect of her children's training ! She was herself highly gifted in practical matters, and she was very anxious that we too should become capable of acting independently, although, as already mentioned, I always had to be under the care of an escort. And just as Mama insisted on great economy in her household affairs, so she trained me too to very great personal simplicity in all matters of dress and habits of life. She wanted above everything else to prevent me from becoming vain, or from thinking myself superior to other girls of my age. It was characteristic, in this connection, that Mama did not even allow people to be presented to me at the first Court ball at Schwerin at which I was present, though it was the general custom for every Princess who came of age.

Punctuality, " the virtue of kings," was one aspect of the code of courtesy by which we were bound. In order to train me to be punctual, Mama always made me go to her five minutes before the time of meals or other appointments. This was a rule for which I am particularly grateful to her when I look back now ; I introduced it again with my own daughters with good results. Above all, however, what Mama required of her children was an unqualified love of truth and the courageous admission of a mistake or transgression ; she on her side was guided by the principle of perfect justice and appealed to her children's intelligence even at an early age. In general the training we had from Mama was extremely strict, but by this she did far more for her children's lives than if she had spoilt and pampered us.

In my sixth year Miss Jenkins' place was taken by a " nursery-governess." The parting from my devoted " Nana " was very hard for me. But as she continued to live in Schwerin I often saw her afterwards. She had a snug little flat in the Alexandrine Palace, opening on to the Old Garden. We used to spend many hours of sociable talk with the old lady, who passed the evening of her life there in peace and undisturbed by anyone. She spoke a quite peculiar blend of German and English, which often contributed to our amusement. Moreover, in spite of her love for her motherland up to the very end, she was filled with loyalty and devotion to Mecklenburg and to our family. She died in the year 1917 at the age of eighty-eight, and is buried in the cemetery at Ludwigslust ; my brother and sister and I regularly visit her grave.

Mrs. Savile, the nursery-governess who took Miss Jenkins' place, was exceptionally good-natured. My instruction in special subjects was in the very capable hands of Fräulein Hildegard Kühne, who had previously taught my brother and sister.

My mother always decided how my day's work was to be apportioned, even to the minutest detail. This was the case even when I was away with my governess, and after every period of absence my mother always had a most detailed report on everything that had taken place, both in my studies and in my everyday life.

In winter, lessons began at 8 o'clock and lasted until 11 or 11.30. My mother was very insistent that I should get a great deal of fresh air, and so I had relatively few lessons during the day. But as they lasted a full hour and I had my lessons alone, I was able to get through the curriculum. After our mid-day meal we would go for a walk or make excursions into the beautiful surrounding country. On ordinary occasions we had tea at 3.30 p.m., lessons from 4 to 6 p.m., and preparation from 6 to 7.30 p.m.

In the year 1898 Fräulein Alwine Vordemann came as my governess, and she also took over my German studies for the most part. In spite of her good qualities, however, I could not get on with her. It was probably because she was no longer young and elastic enough to treat me, as a young girl, in such a way as to establish successful relations between teacher and pupil. But she was very well-read and took an active interest in the theatre, which was to be of considerable benefit to me in my later visits to Dresden. Fräulein Vordemann stayed only two years, as my mother was afraid that too frequent conflicts might be bad for my character.

Pastor Ehrich gave me my first religious instruction. He had been my brother's tutor for several years, at the same time giving us sisters lessons in several subjects. His cheerful temperament, and the friendly way in which he dealt with our individualities and even entered into our little jokes, especially endeared him to us children. Pastor Ehrich is now provost of the church at Ludwigslust. We can still enjoy with him the dear

memories of the past, and laugh heartily at the long forgotten stories of our childhood which he tells to perfection. How nice it is, and how it warms the heart, to feel
that we are linked by lasting ties of friendship with those
who were with us in our childhood !

Later on, my religious instruction was given me by
Pastor Hermann Schmidt, who had the care of souls
in the little German church at Cannes. He filled this
office for thirty years, to the spiritual benefit of so many
Germans at Cannes, in spite of the fact that he himself
was very weak in health and had to fight against asth-
matic trouble. He could not even preach standing up,
but had to sit on a tall arm-chair in the pulpit. His loyal
fulfilment of his duty and his self-sacrifice should be an
example to all. His assistant ministers or the vicar of the
church helped him in giving religious instruction. Vicar
Alberts, the present Superintendent at Stendal, probably
came most in contact with me, and I have since kept
actively in touch with him.

My French studies, which had to receive special attention owing to the fact that we spent half the year at
Cannes, were in the very best hands with Mlle. Leonie
Pascon. I had the good luck to be her pupil for many
years—even after my engagement I continued my literature studies with her—and I learnt a great deal from this
estimable and cultured lady, for which I have been
grateful to her all my life. Her whole teaching was
remarkable for its precision and thoroughness. In the
process of learning the language I was brought into contact with French literature and art and also the history

HM   113

of the country. In her teaching of history she used the very good method of making me follow the development of the most important States by comparative treatment. We drew up tables on this basis which were very clear and widened one's horizon. Her stimulating text-books gave me a thorough understanding of the various epochs. We also read the French classics, which both in form and content seemed to me to be extraordinarily instructive as an expression of the period. It is a matter of great regret to me that the passage of years has blotted out much of this knowledge. For literature, art and history are spiritual treasures which can only be fully and usefully appreciated in later years.

In the year 1909, when I went to Cannes on the occasion of my grandfather's death, I saw Mlle. Pascon for the last time. She had not changed at all and had lost none of her cordial interest in me and in my future life. She noted, however, to her regret, that my pronunciation and fluency in speaking French had suffered from lack of practice. Mlle. Pascon died before the war, so that there was never any estrangement between us, such as intervened unfortunately in my relations with many others who were subjects of enemy countries.

From the time that I was quite small I was taught drawing and painting, and probably had a certain gift, especially for landscapes ; the time which I spent in Dresden, when I was able to take drawing lessons together with my brother, had a specially stimulating effect on me. Unfortunately I made very little use of this talent later on, and I regret more than anything else that I did not go further in water-colour painting, which particularly suited me ; for an original water-colour study of Nature is a charming object, and gives genuine satisfaction to the painter. Unfortunately, too, as a child I went far too seldom to picture galleries and museums except when I was in Dresden; for the eye has to be trained early to acquire an understanding of paint-ings and works of art. My mother always thought that there would be time enough for that when I grew up. So to my regret I never in my youth visited Italy for the purposes of study, although I was so near ; it would certainly have been very helpful in my education.

I took piano lessons with great zeal. In Schwerin I was taught by Herr Romberg, who was for many years in charge of the choir in the castle chapel ; and at Cannes by the very accomplished piano teacher Madame Verne, who had a wide knowledge of German and classical music. She made me practise according to the methods of the Czerny and Pleyel schools, and after I had mastered some sonatinas she made me play several Beethoven sonatas. What I learned with her I have never forgotten ; I am sincerely grateful to her for the thorough grounding which she gave me.

When distinguished musicians came to Cannes it gave me the greatest pleasure to be allowed to attend their concerts. Unfortunately I never heard the famous weekly symphony concerts in the Casino at Monte Carlo, because my mother did not want to let me go into the Casino. But a concert which the Berlin Philharmonic Orchestra gave one winter at Cannes was one of the great events of my childhood. It was on that occasion that I heard Beethoven's immortal " Seventh " for the first time. I was completely absorbed in the glorious music of this masterpiece, which from that time, so to say, has accompanied me through life like a close friend.

The great passion which I have for classical music was aroused in me at an early age. I also liked operas, and my frequent visits to Dresden gave the best possible opportunity to attend first-class performances. But I was only allowed to visit the opera once in each week so that in Dresden, where I used to stay about three weeks, I only managed to hear three operas at most during each visit, the object being to prevent me from becoming bored with them. I mention this to show how precise were the instructions by which my life was governed by my mother, even from afar. There was only one occasion on which, in response to an urgent request from my grandfather, I was given permission to exceed the number of visits to the opera which had been laid down. But how my greedy eyes and ears delighted in the sensations of such an evening !

I can say that even in my early years I had already learnt to appreciate good technique in music. Many of the then famous singers of the Dresden Opera left a deep impression on me. I went less frequently to plays ; the *Jungfrau von Orleans* comes to my mind—I saw it at Schwerin at one of its early performances with Fräulein Wohlgemuth, who is now at the Burg theatre in Vienna, as Joan of Arc.

In Dresden, too, under the direction of Councillor

Jakob, I learnt to recite poetry with correct expression. Councillor Jakob was the type of the courtly humanistic scholar—one could have imagined him very well in the rococo period, in pumps and wearing a queue—and at the same time he was very kind-hearted and had exceptional ability. He gave my brother lessons in the German language when he was at school, first at the Vitztum Gymnasium, and afterwards as a private pupil, and was of considerable help to my brother in developing his outstanding talent as a speaker.

From an early age I was very fond of reading, and as my mother gave me every Christmas some beautiful books, which she selected in consultation with my governess, I only had good things to read in my youth. Historical romances were what I liked best. I devoured with the greatest avidity Walter Scott's writings, and had a great enthusiasm for his heroes. I was also very fond of Gustav Freytag's *Die Ahnen*. Mama was very cautious over modern novels—and what peculiar works were then described as modern !—but she allowed me to read some of them. I remember one of these novels, Ompteda's *Heimat des Herzens*, which made a great impression on me because of the conflict with which it dealt—the union of two people who belonged to different nations. The historical figure which most attracted me was the Staufenhausen Emperor Friedrich II. What pleasure it gave me last year to be able, in my mature years, to study Kantorowicz's fine work, and to find the hero of my youth so vividly and profoundly conceived !

In December 1900 Fräulein Vordemann left me, and

her place was taken by Fräulein Lucie King who came from St. Petersburg, where she had been teaching for some years at the Imperial Gymnasium. She was descended from what had been originally a Norman family, and through her mother she had German and Italian blood in her veins. Her Russian manner was adopted, but for that reason was all the more pronounced. Fräulein King spoke four languages fluently, but German best of the four, and her cultural outlook too was German in spite of her Italian vivacity, her English energy and her essentially Russian warm-heartedness. Clever and penetrating, but at the same time honest and straightforward, she never made a secret of her opinions and sentiments and always said quite openly what she meant. She was often in sharp disagreement with my mother, but this did not produce any conflict, because they each appreciated the other's standpoint too well. My further mental development was in the hands of this self-sacrificing woman from then until my marriage ; she was my constant companion, my adviser in all educational matters and in my various hobbies, and above all truly maternal in her devotion.

My mother devoted much of her time to games and social functions, and in consequence of this she could only have me with her to a limited extent ; and moreover we were frequently separated from each other by longer or shorter intervals of absence. It was therefore only natural, in spite of all the guiding principles laid down by my mother, that Fräulein King developed complete independence of mind in her educational methods and because of this she also won an influence which was to a high degree decisive in my development and my whole conception of life.

She guided me through all those years with a hand which was both gentle and firm, and her most fundamental principle was that I must be kept on the path of unconditional veracity and the fulfilment of duty down to the minutest detail. If perhaps she sometimes showed a certain indulgence in relation to my vivacious and susceptible temperament, this was only the expression of her tender motherly heart, of her feeling that I was a child growing up without companions and that I needed warmth and affection. Thus at the very beginning of our acquaintance she won my heart by nursing me lovingly through an illness, and a relationship which can only be described as friendship was soon established between us. She has retained this deep affection for me up to the present day, and I feel that I can never recompense her for what she gave me out of her overflowing heart.

Fräulein King drew up a careful and extensive scheme for my education, and this was approved by my mother. She herself undertook Russian and English, until Mr. Jackson, my brother's tutor, became available when my brother came of age, and then he gave me English lessons for two years. He was an Afrikander by birth, and a violin player until an injury to his hand forced him to change his profession. In the year 1903 he married Fräulein von Oertzen, who was then one of the ladies of the Court. Fräulein Katherina Schröter, of Potsdam, who was governess in the Kockritz-Stirum household, was appointed to teach me German, History, Geography and Mathematics. She was very nice, and very cultured and musical ; I still have a sincere respect for her.

The last winter before my confirmation was the most important period in my studies. For it was then a question of bringing everything I had learnt on to a higher plane. With this aim in view a teacher was sought who could concentrate on giving me an insight into social-historical studies. Dr. Köhler was selected ; he had worked for a long time with Professor Lamprecht, the sociologist, in Leipzig. Dr. Köhler's lessons were very interesting, and were almost like little lectures. I have to thank him for many stimulating surveys, and I am particularly indebted to him for the great trouble which he took with me. Dr. Köhler stayed until my confirmation, and even came to stay at Schwerin with us.

Pastor Schmidt, who has already been mentioned, gave me special instruction for two winters leading up to my confirmation. For these lessons I used to go to his comfortable quarters above the German church, where he lived with his niece, Fräulein Warneyer, who kept house for him. The hours spent with this old gentleman were very beautiful and enjoyable. Then at Schwerin from the middle of May 1903, the first chaplain of the Court, Dr. Wolff, prepared me finally for confirmation. These final lessons were of the greatest importance for my religious development, for they made me acquainted with the positive Lutheran creed ; it was certainly not easy for me to understand it, but I found the exposition

THE RUSSIAN GRANDPARENTS OF THE AUTHORESS

GRAND DUCHESS OLGA FEODOROVNA
née PRINCESS OF BADEN

GRAND DUKE MICHAIL NIKOLAIEVICH

of it completely convincing. Pastor Wolff is still a benevolent friend and spiritual adviser to my brother and
sister and myself, and we miss no opportunity of going
to see him in Schwerin and telling him how fate is dealing
with our lives.

*

My mother was always striving to make me win knowledge not only from dead books but from living observation. It was from this standpoint that even my travels
were arranged, as there is probably no better means of
achieving real education than judicious travel, carefully
prepared beforehand. This is why I am particularly
grateful to my mother for letting me visit the World
Exhibition at Paris in the year 1900. Fräulein King and
I were there for several days and saw the most important
sections; the *Palais d'arts*, with its glorious artistic exhibits,
gave me the greatest pleasure. I vividly remember, too,
an ascent we made of the Eiffel Tower and a visit
to the *Trottoir roulant*. The beautiful city was in itself an
incomparable experience, with its wide avenues, the
Champs Élysées, and the great streams of traffic. The
great dark structure of the Louvre, with the Tuileries,
made the greatest impression on me because they
recalled the imperial and royal splendour of the past,
and my thoughts were fully occupied with those who
had formerly dwelt in these palaces, especially Marie
Antoinette and Napoleon—and even at that time such
reflections made me extremely melancholy !

I have retained in my mind one other picture of Paris :

the Place de la Concorde, where the Strassburg statue, draped in black, was a daily reminder to the French of the city which they had lost in 1870–71. One can only think with shame that with us there is nowhere to be found any monument to the tragic memory of the territories which were German to the core and were torn from us at Versailles !

In the spring of each year I used to go to Switzerland with my governess for a stay of a few weeks, this being intended to provide a transition from the warmth of the south to the climate of the north.

On several of these journeys we travelled to Lucerne or the Lake of Geneva, where on one occasion I stayed at Vevey and on another at beautiful Glion, high above the waters of the Lake. The wide meadows, completely covered with narcissus, absolutely enchanted me. The trip up to Caux on the cog-wheel railway was also a great delight ; to find deep snow there in May was to me an unaccustomed and therefore all the more astonishing sight, as I was only used to the warm south. My visit to Chillon Castle, which is linked with the legend of the " prisoner " who, according to Lord Byron, languished in chains for many years in the castle dungeons, actively excited my imagination. The Dent du Midi, which with its seven peaks towers over the valley of the Rhône, formed a magnificent background to this glorious landscape. Once, too, we went to Bozen, where we were able to admire the rose garden in the Alpine glow.

But interesting and educative as these journeys were, nevertheless their charm was spoilt by the fact that I could find no peace of mind. For I was irresistibly drawn towards my long-desired country of Mecklenburg, from which I had had to be absent the whole winter through. Besides, we were hardly able to undertake any very extensive outings, because our allowance for the journey was very strictly limited. For, as I have already empha- sised, my mother insisted that our everyday mode of life should be extremely economical, and even when travel- ling we were not allowed to relax this principle.

The weeks which I spent, for many summers in succes- sion, at my brother's pretty villa in Dresden, in the Mosczinskystrasse, at the corner of the Beuststrasse, were incomparably delightful. My brother lived with his tutors, Herr Viktor von Köckritz and Mr. Frank Jackson ; the latter had been with him for many years, and, as I mentioned earlier, afterwards taught me also. Fräulein Vordemann and I used our spare time for frequent walks through the enchantingly beautiful town, to make purchases and also to visit the galleries and museums. Apart from the picture gallery in the citadel I particularly liked the Johanneum porcelain collection, and my repeated visits there were probably responsible for developing my partiality for fine porce- lain.

My brother brought his carriage and horses with him from Schwerin, and so on our free afternoons we were able to take short drives in the gardens or to go for longer excursions through the far-spreading Dresden woodlands, magnificent pine forests which tower above the high eastern bank of the Elbe. On a drive with

Fräulein Vordemann we once saw, not far from the town, the memorial to the French General Moreau who, then in the service of Russia, was mortally wounded in the Battle of Dresden. It astonished me to hear that only his legs, which had been shot off, are buried under his memorial, while he himself was buried in Petersburg.

Visits which we paid to two old ladies are still vivid in my mind. One of them was Frau von Bornemann, who had been born in Mecklenburg and had known our grandparents. Her husband had been for many years Mecklenburg's ambassador at the Court of the Emperor Napoleon III, and she could tell enthralling stories of her experiences there. The other was the aged Countess Versen, *née* von Rauch, niece of the famous sculptor, whose father had been Adjutant-General in the Russian service under Tsar Nikolai I. She too had been brought up at the Russian Court, and had been an intimate friend of my great-grandmother, the Tsarina Charlotte. She could give very interesting accounts of people and conditions at the Court of the Tsar ; when later on I read the extremely interesting reminiscences written by Dr. Mandts, who had been physician in ordinary to Tsar Nikolai I, I was vividly reminded of the accounts given by Countess Versen.

In Dresden we used to make particularly frequent visits to the Schönburg house in the Wienerstrasse, where Princess Lucie of Schönburg-Waldenburg, *née* Princess Wittgenstein, lived with her daughter Sophie, who afterwards became Princess Wilhelm of Wied and Princess of Albania, and her two sons Otto Viktor and

Günther. I soon made friends with Sophie and spent many very pleasant and interesting hours in their hospitable home. Otto Viktor was afterwards killed right at the beginning of the world war, when he was serving in France with the Guards. He was in charge of a patrol and had ridden up to the railway embankment by the village of Fresnes to reconnoitre, drawing the fire of the marksmen concealed behind the embankment, who recognised by his flowing cloak that he was an officer. He fell from his horse with a bullet through his heart, and the young prince breathed his last lying under a rosebush. His last words were to tell his troops not to endanger their own lives on his account.

In our gay circle at Dresden there were also the sons of Count Fritz Hohenau, who were attending the Vitzthum Gymnasium, and Adolf Friedrich, then heir to the Grand Duke of Mecklenburg-Strelitz, who was also studying in Dresden and had been an intimate friend of my brother from his childhood up. He was a sympathetic well-bred young man, but probably too gentle for this hard world, and so to our great sorrow he came to such a tragic end in 1918.

From time to time we made joint excursions into the extremely beautiful country round Dresden ; one merry outing to the Switzerland of Saxony is still particularly vivid in my mind. After a long ramble we had supper at Schandau, and then began the homeward journey in very merry spirits. Finally the highest point of our amusement was reached in a regular battle in the train, during which we of the weaker sex had to take refuge in the corners of the compartment so as to escape injury.

It was an exceptional experience for me, accustomed as I was to live as a rule all by myself and rather quietly to have the opportunity to be with so many jolly and high-spirited young people. It came to an end in the year 1900, when my brother went to Bonn and his household at Dresden was broken up. But I still went again and again to Dresden to be with my grandfather, the Grand Duke Michail Nikolaievich, who took a cure there every year from the late autumn until early in December.

Fräulein King and I lived with my grandfather at the Bellevue, which is gloriously situated on the Elbe ; we were very comfortable there, thanks to the careful management of the proprietor, Ronnefeld. As a rule Fräulein King and I had rooms looking out towards the opera-house. This gave me indescribable pleasure, for I loved the Dresden opera with all the glowing enthusiasm of a schoolgirl. At noon I could see the opera-singers, men and women, going home after the rehearsals ; at other times of the day the scenery would be changed, or instruments brought in : everything connected with the operas I loved was of burning interest to me !

And what were my feelings as I sat in the box on the occasion when I was allowed to go to a performance ! Impatient and full of excitement I would keep looking at the peculiar square clock in the auditorium, on which hours and minutes appeared as figures in squares and went out of sight with a sudden downward jerk. This clock was a special delight to me, and I always greeted it as an old friend. It is still a pleasure to me to recall the magnificent performances of *Tannhäuser*, *Lohengrin*, *Don Juan*, *Die verkaufte Braut*, *Rienzi* and other operas. Once, too, I heard a wonderful symphony concert with my mother in the opera-house. Artistes such as Therese Malten, Marie Wittich, Frau Abendroth, Erika Wedekind, and the tenor Karl Burrian, the baritone Karl Scheidemantel, Friedrich Plaschke and others are still vivid in my mind.

In the director's box we often saw Count Seebach, who made Dresden one of the chief centres of modern theatrical life, for plays and operas, by his courageous organisation of many first performances, with the support of a brilliant company. I first made his acquaintance in 1917, when I was once again in Dresden. On that occasion, as Crown Princess I was received by him and conducted to the royal box, while as a child or schoolgirl I was a " private individual " and sat almost unnoticed in one of the comfortable boxes in the dress circle.

Apart from these rare evenings life in Dresden passed very quietly. After meals I played halma with my grandfather. There, too, I first recited to him a long Russian poem on Mount Kazbek, the highest mountain in the Caucasus. In spite of stage-fright and the violent beating of my heart it went off quite well, and my grandfather was extremely pleased with the progress I had made in the Russian language.

Sometimes my grandfather was visited by the Arch-duchess Maria Theresa, sister-in-law of the Emperor

Franz Josef. These visits were a great pleasure to both of them, as they were very much in sympathy with each other. The Archduchess was of distinguished appearance and very lovable, in which she resembled her sister, Marie José, the Countess Karl Theodor of Bavaria. I remember how the Archduchess once came to the hotel on a surprise visit, without having let us know that she was coming. We met her on the stairs, and my grandfather embraced the Archduchess and kissed her, in the Russian way, three times on her cheeks—to the no small astonishment of the hotel servants who were about !

My grandfather also took me with him on his visits to Strehlin to see Queen Carola, wife of King Albert of Saxony ; she was a very nice motherly woman. I can still recall that my grandfather used to have intense conversations with her on serious and religious matters, and that in the course of these they touched on the sects which were then gaining ground in South Russia. On our last visit other members of the Saxon royal family were also present, including the Crown Princess Luise, who kindly devoted her attention to me as I was a young girl. She was very pretty and vivacious and extraordinarily natural in her manner. Six weeks later she left Dresden and her family for ever.

Through my visits to my brother and my grandfather Dresden became almost like my home, and I am never in that beautiful city without experiencing a feeling of being at home and the grateful memory of the happy days I spent there in my youth. A few years ago on the way from München to Oels I once more visited Dresden,

VILLA WENDEN

and strolled quite by myself along the streets through which I had so often passed as a child. They were still quite quiet and empty, as it was Sunday and early in the morning. The Mosczinskystrasse, where my brother used to live, had hardly changed at all. The villa, which belonged to Chief Equerry von Haugk, who died during the war, looks almost exactly the same as it did thirty years ago. It gave me a strange feeling to have this fleeting glimpse, as a grown-up person and in such altered circumstances, of the streets which had been so familiar to me in my childhood.

*

July 3, 1903 was the solemn day of my confirmation. On the previous day I had been examined in the presence of my mother, my brother and Miss King. I had been quite sure of myself in answering all the many questions which were put to me, so that I could go calmly and happily to the beautiful ceremony that awaited me the next day.

It was a glorious day of brilliant sunshine. Roses in full bloom nodded in at the window of my room, the waters of the lake murmured softly round our beloved family castle, and my home all round me was decked in its loveliest ! I shall never forget the solemn moment when my mother and my brother led me from the hall out to the castle chapel, where I took my place in front of the altar. Many of my relations and members of the Court were already assembled. But I soon forgot their presence and, with grateful heart, looked up at the coloured windows, through which the sun was streaming, and at the marble image of Christ which watches over the beautiful altar. Here too I was able to get through the long examination which was customary in Mecklenburg ; deeply moved, I knelt at the altar and prayed that the blessing of the Lord might descend on me. I had myself chosen the text which the first chaplain of the Court, Doctor Wolff, pronounced : " Commend thy ways unto the Lord and trust in Him, He will give thee strength." It has solaced me all through my life.

At the close of the ceremony I joined the royal group, from now on one of its " grown-up " members, escorted by my cousin Paul Friedrich ; in my mother's salon a table loaded with presents was waiting for me. After the family breakfast I was presented to the Court assembled in the hall, and with a full heart I received many affectionate congratulations.

In the evening we drove to Ludwigslust, in order to participate next morning in the Communion service at my beloved father's grave. We sat near his sarcophagus in the wonderful white mausoleum, which is almost festal in its appearance. My brother and sister, my brother-in-law Christian and my godfather Heinrich XVIII Reuss went with me to the altar. My mother, as a member of the Orthodox Church, and Miss King who belonged to the Reformed Church, did not take Communion, but they were with me in the closest spiritual sympathy. This first Communion at the grave of my father made a lasting impression upon me. Many years later, when our elder sons were confirmed at Potsdam, this solemn ceremony was repeated in the Old Temple at the tomb of my children's beloved grandmother, Kaiserin Auguste Viktoria.

With my confirmation my education was officially completed, although my former teacher remained with me and my studies continued. Fräulein King received the title of a maid of honour, as my mother did not yet wish me to have a lady-in-waiting. She herself did not want to let me go out into the world so soon, and for a long time to come insisted on my childish dependence upon her maternal guidance.

CHAPTER VI

SUMMER VISITS TO RUSSIA

When one has spent many glad and happy days with a dear friend and then sees him die in circumstances of unutterable sadness, and sees everything which bore witness to his life and work systematically and utterly destroyed, then one is loth to rouse these memories again—from fear that they might once more open the old scars of pain which as yet have hardly healed.

That is how I feel when I set myself the task of recounting those impressions of Russia which once brought me such a wealth of happiness and had such a deep influence on my early years. Our annual journey there, my life in the house of my dear grandfather, the Grand Duke Michail Nikolaievich, the realisation of the vast, world-encircling might of Imperial Russia at that period, contact with people and with things whose roots lay in those immeasurable spaces—all these built up in my youthful mind a conception of something indestructible and almighty, which must in some way hang together with the existence of the earth. That the Russian Empire could ever be dissolved would have seemed to me just as unthinkable as that the earth might come into collision with the moon and disappear from the universe.

And I gained these impressions directly from the Imperial Court itself; as a near relation of the Tsar's

132

family I absorbed them with enthusiastic susceptibility. At the same time I must say in advance that naturally I was never in a position to gain any intimate knowledge of Russian conditions and of Russian people such as those portrayed by Dostoievski ; but nevertheless I saw at first hand the gigantic apparatus of Russia's administrative machine, and I heard a great deal from my relatives, who were able to form a very precise estimate of the position. My mother's eldest brother, Nikolai Michailovich, was particularly well informed ; he was regarded as the most liberal of the Grand Dukes, and because of his many-sided interests he came in contact with circles which would otherwise have had nothing to do with the Court. I have already mentioned that during his winter visits to Cannes he used willingly to tell me about his historical studies.

I experienced personally so much affection and kindness in Russia that the feeling of gratitude for it is still inextinguishable in my heart. It moves me deeply when even now, after everything that has happened to Russia and Germany, I meet with so much loyalty and trust on the part of Russian emigrants. Of course I cannot ascribe this to myself personally, but to the great love which my grandfather enjoyed in the Russian Empire, and to the respect felt for my mother among her countrymen.

*

From 1898 to 1904 I went to Russia every summer with my mother. My grandfather lived in his country house, Michailovskoe, which lay between Strelna and

· Peterhof on Kronstadt Bay, perhaps half-an-hour's train journey from St. Petersburg.

Our journey, which we usually made by sea, was in itself very enjoyable. As a rule the Grand Duke Alexei, as Grand Admiral or Chief Commander of the Russian Fleet, despatched the big armoured cruiser *Svietlana*, of 3,800 tons, which was at his disposal as a personal yacht, to one of the Baltic ports to fetch my mother. On two occasions also Tsar Nikolai placed his beautiful yacht *Standard* at her disposal for the return voyage, an act of courtesy to a Grand Duchess who has married outside her country which is probably without parallel.

The *Standard* was a three-master steam yacht with a black hull ; she was a magnificent vessel with a clipper bow, which made her look very smart. The internal arrangements were comparatively simple, but very comfortable and practical. The Tsar and Tsarina had a liking for birch and maple wood, and for flowery cretonnes or washable chintzes, and evidence of this was on every side.

When the *Standard* on one occasion brought us to Warnemünde, a group of officers came from there to Gelbensande to visit us, on Mama's invitation. Their entries in the visitors' book are still there to-day to remind us of our former beautiful journeys by sea to Russia.

But if no ship was available, a royal train would be sent for us to the frontier at Eydtkuhnen. These royal trains, and more particularly the older ones, were fitted

out with the utmost luxury, and the deep upholstered
sofas and chairs of the saloon carriage were covered with
silk damask. We had an undisturbed sleep on a proper
bed in the sleeping compartments. The trains used to
run very slowly and therefore with very little jolting,
which made the journey a very pleasant one. The loco-
motives were even heated with wood so that the travel-
lers should not be annoyed by coal-dust. The excellent
food, characteristic of the Tsar's Court, was another advantage of the royal train which was not to be under-
estimated.

There was interest enough to be got from the 24 to 36
hours' journey which had to be made through the great
Russian Empire. The few towns which we touched,
Vilna, Pskov, and other smaller places, all looked the
same : mostly wooden houses, Russian churches with
onion-shaped towers, and military guards at the sta-
tions. But apart from these there were the wide, boundless moors, forests of birch and pine, meadows with round
pointed hay-ricks such are still to be found with us in
Lusatia, stretches of water on whose surface the setting
sun glowed red, and now and then villages of log-houses,
and almost nowhere a cultivated cornfield. It was all infinitely melancholy, but at the same time indescribably
attractive. For what a long time after these journeys this
landscape would still be influencing my childish imagination ! In the Gelbensande forest, when a chill autumn
breeze brought the yellow beech-leaves twirling down,
how I often found myself travelling in spirit to Russia,
to its desolate places, its boundless plains ! The white

135

trunks of birches, mossy ground and autumn melancholy still bring back to me the picture of the Russian landscape.

But beautiful as were the rail journeys through the Russian plain, they were far excelled by the sea journeys. To my mother and myself these were a constant source of pleasure. And although on bright nights in the middle of summer the voyage through the Baltic as far as Kronstadt was specially delightful, how much more delightful it used to be on that comfortably-appointed yacht, with all the attention and kindness paid to us by the Russian admirals and officers! It is true that when I made the voyage for the first time I was surrounded by people who hardly spoke anything but Russian, and I felt very helpless because I did not know a word of Russian myself. But this feeling wore off more and more each year, as my knowledge of the Russian language improved.

How interesting even going on board was for someone who had never before made a voyage on a warship! First the officers were presented, a ceremony in which I was allowed to participate. Then followed the greeting of the crew. For this, the crew was lined up round the decks, and my mother, escorted by the captain, walked down the line and greeted the sailors with " Zdorovo Bratsa ! " (Good health to you, brothers !) to which they replied with a full-throated " Zdorovie jelaem, Vashe Imperatorskoe Visotshestvo ! " (We wish good health to Your Imperial Highness !)

If the ship was lying at Swinemünde or in Warnemünde

GRAND DUCHESS ANASTASIA WITH PRINCE BISMARCK AT FRIEDRICHSRUH

roads, the anchor would be raised soon after our arrival. But when we joined her at Kiel, we would make some visit in the harbour during the evening. My most memorable experience on such an occasion was a visit to the *Hohenzollern* when she was once lying in Kiel Harbour with the Kaiser and Kaiserin on board. To our surprise the Kaiser with a large retinue was waiting for us at the station, and took us straight off in his graceful launch to see the Kaiserin. It was the first time I was presented to my future parents-in-law ; it was on this occasion too that I met my future brother-in-law Adalbert, the first of the Crown Prince's brothers whose acquaintance I made.

On the *Hohenzollern* there was first the usual exchange of greetings with the officers and the leading members of the Kaiser's retinue. Then the Kaiserin received my mother with her ladies in the ante-room of the dining-saloon, and after that we went down into the saloon, where an animated conversation took place. The Kaiser had paid an early visit to the *Svietlana* ; she had just arrived and the decks had not yet been cleared. He told us very gaily of the surprise which his early visit had caused, and that even at that early hour a good deal of vodka had been consumed. The Kaiserin was very kind and friendly even to a schoolgirl as I was then, and I remember that when they talked about her sailing-yacht *Iduna* I could not help observing that I thought the name a very pretty one. Then I blushed deeply at having broken in with my remark, but I had the impression that Their Majesties were not vexed with me for it.

What beautiful memories bind us with the *Iduna*, that lovely sailing-yacht ! Later on the Kaiserin often placed her at our disposal. The first long voyage we made in her was after my marriage ; we went first on the *Meteor*, the Kaiser's racing-yacht, and then when the *Meteor* had to leave for the Cowes regatta we changed over to the *Iduna*. With Captain Karpf in command we had a glorious cruise through Danish waters to Bornholm and then on to Swinemünde. The last time I was on the *Iduna* I was with my son Wilhelm, who was then quite small but already very keen on the sea ; we made a cruise from Danzig to Bornholm, Heiligendamm and Warnemünde. In 1914 my brother-in-law Eitel Friedrich and his wife were overtaken by the imminent danger of war when they were at Stockholm in the course of a peaceful cruise on the *Iduna*. Now that beautiful white ship, which in full sail resembled a haughty swan, has been sold to America, and those lovely cruises on our own vessel, like so much else, belong to the past. But in those days I had no idea of what the future held, and revelled in what was to my girlish mind the enchanting present.

After our visit to the *Hohenzollern* the Kaiser accompanied us to the *Svietlana* and bade us an extremely friendly farewell. I was very proud of his having helped me out of the boat in his knightly way, and of his having called me " my daughter." Who could then have guessed that one day I should have a right to be called that !

The voyage to Kronstadt took a day and a half or two days, according to the port from which we started. As a rule the weather was fine and still, which of course is a necessary condition for a pleasant trip. How wonderful it was when night descended on the sea, slowly and at quite a late hour ! What depth there was in the blue darkness of the shimmering sky and sea, as I looked out of the cabin window before going to sleep, and how sublime was the impression made on me by the calm expanse of sea !

I lay in my cabin listening to the continuous lapping of the water against the ship's side, supremely happy to be on board such a lovely ship, and looking forward to the glorious days and weeks ahead. Was it truth or a dream ? A feeling that it was unreal rose in me. To convince myself that I was not in a dream my eyes always sought the familiar image of Christ which hung in a corner of the cabin. For orthodox custom required that here too, as in every room in which people lived, there should be an ikon.

Every evening at sunset there was an extremely impressive ceremony on Russian ships of war : the hauling down of the flag and the service appropriate to it. The crew formed up in a square on deck, and the priest in a gold-embroidered vestment stood in the middle and recited a prayer. At the moment when the sun sank into the sea the roll of the drums sounded, the flag was lowered from the mast, and the band played " Ich bete an die Macht der Liebe," while the officers and crew stood bareheaded in deep devotion. Words cannot describe the solemnity of the proceedings. The sea lay calm and still. The horizon glowed in the last rays of the setting sun. The outline of a sailing vessel rose like a ghost out of the twilight. One could feel the even rhythm of the engines of our ship. My youthful soul was deeply moved, and was completely under the spell of this marvellous moment.

It all created an impression on me which I shall never lose through life.

We took our meals with the captain in his beautiful dining-room aft. The Russian food was excellent, if perhaps rather rich. At noon each day the crew's food was sampled which meant that a sailor would ceremonially offer a plate to my mother, a plate to me, to the captain and the others, for us to taste. On the second evening we were usually invited to the comfortable officers' mess and spent a pleasant evening in this friendly company ; in the course of years we got to know them well, as the senior officers were seldom transferred to other ships. On these occasions we were offered tea in glasses with a slice of lemon and also Russian sweetmeats. Several of the officers played the piano or sang Russian songs, most of which were melancholy. But nicest of all was the balalaika orchestra, which sat at the open door and played their rhythmical melodies. In Russia practically every large ship and probably every regiment had such a balalaika orchestra, and also singers who were exceptionally well trained. Russians are by nature extraordinarily musical.

In the early morning, cheered by the sun and the deep blue-green of the sea, we went up on the bridge, and from there looked out at ships or at the coast when it

came into view. On one occasion we dropped anchor
at Rügen, and my brother, who was with us, went ashore
with some officers in the launch and landed at the cliffs
by Arcona, where there was a naval station. They handed
in telegrams and inspected the lighthouse.

All kinds of deck games were organised for our entertainment. One of these was " Bull," something like a
game that is now played on all ocean liners ; a long piece
of sail-cloth is spread out, with black squares in which
numbers were painted. The players formed two sides,
and had to try to throw fairly heavy rings, made of
twisted tow, into the squares. The side which at the end
of the game had scored the highest total was the winner.
But nicest of all was a proper slide made of boards and
fixed at a slope from a part of the superstructure. We sat
on a little carpet at the top, and then, highly delighted,
tobogganed down the slide and, because of the momen-
tum we had gathered, a little way along the deck, which
was waxed for the purpose. Other forms of entertainment were the dances performed by the sailors, and the
games they played, at which we were spectators. In all
of this the Russian sailors gave an impression of good-
nature and loyalty ; their relations with their superiors
also seemed to be very good.

On the second day of the voyage we came into sight of
Reval. This old town, which still looks as if it belongs to
the Middle Ages, is profoundly impressive when seen
from the sea, with its churches and towers. The cathedral recalls the German past of this Hanseatic city, while
the Orthodox Alexander-Nevski Cathedral with its

gilded cupolas bears testimony to the more recent rule of Russia over the Baltic countries.

It was an extremely interesting experience for me when, on one of our voyages, we were able to be present at the Russian naval manœuvres. We saw torpedo-boat attacks and the defence against them, and other tactical manœuvres which were thrilling and instructive to a high degree.

When we got up early on the third day we were generally already lying in the roads at Kronstadt, the fortress which lies on an island in the Gulf of Finland. As we came in we received a salute from the old-fashioned forts, which date from the time when Russia was engaged in a naval war with Sweden ; their massive dark-grey walls gave the fortress a curiously sinister and menacing appearance. The modern batteries which commanded the entrance to Kronstadt Bay were built on piles in the water and looked as if they were floating on the sea.

The Grand Duke Alexei often came to Kronstadt to welcome us. He was a giant in stature, more like Tsar Alexander III than any of his other brothers ; he was very vivacious, with a loud voice, and very friendly and jovial. Prince Urusoff, too, always reported himself to my mother and was at her service for the duration of her visit ; he was a good friend to us, and his daughter was a close friend of my sister. The commandant of Kronstadt also came on board to greet my mother, and sometimes too my dear grandfather himself. On such occasions there was always an indescribable display of affection, and his joy at our arrival was positively moving to behold.

Then we had to take our leave of the *Svietlana* and prepare for the trip across Kronstadt Bay to Peterhof. We went on board the *Strela* (Arrow), a slim little yacht which served the Tsar's family as a means of transport between Peterhof and St. Petersburg. When we cast off, the band played and the guns of the *Svietlana* fired a salute, and it was with a certain feeling of regret that after a while we saw the ship of which we had grown so fond disappear on the horizon.

But soon new impressions came to occupy our attention. The coast drew closer, Oranienbaum became distinct, and it was not long before Peterhof too came into view. If my grandfather had not come to meet us at Kronstadt he would be waiting for us at the landing-stage at Peterhof, accompanied by my uncles and his staff. After a hearty exchange of greetings we were conducted to the carriage, and then the lively Orloff trotters, which would already be impatiently pawing the ground, began to pull and went off at a rapid trot—the sound of their hoofs on the wide stage of logs covered with plank, was like the roll of a drum. Then we passed at a rapid pace through the lovely park of Peterhof, with the Great Palace on the right, and on through the gate of the strongly guarded Alexandria Park, where Their Majesties were then in residence. The officers of the watch threw open the gates and stood stiffly at the present while we rushed through, and on we went past wide meadows, beautiful groves and idyllic little houses in cottage style ; then out again into the public part of the park, along by the Snamenskaia and the rambling red castle of the Grand Dukes Peter and Nikolai Nikolaie-vich, and then after a further half-hour's drive we turned in to the park of Michailovskoe. Here again for a while we drove past meadows and birches, then past the quar-ters of the staff, until finally we reached the end of our journey : Michailovskoe Castle lay before us, and many of our dear relatives with my grandfather's retinue and attendants—all old friends of my mother from her child-hood—were standing there to give us a most hearty welcome.

CHAPTER VII

MICHAILOVSKOE, MY MOTHER'S HOME

Michailovskoe, my grandfather's summer residence, lay in a charming and idyllic position on the Gulf of Finland, by the side of the wide road along the coast which leads from St. Petersburg through Strelna to Peterhof and Oranienbaum, past parks and villas and the country-seats of other Grand Dukes. As is well-known, Peterhof, the Russian Versailles, was the summer residence of the Tsar's family, and Michailovskoe itself was a white house in the southern style, with a great many verandas and terraces and doors giving direct access to the park.

My mother always occupied the rooms in one of the wings which had been hers as a girl : a great salon, communicating with the garden through several glass doors, and a small bedroom. Next to her was her youngest brother, my uncle Sergei.

At the end were my grandparents' rooms. They were long and wide, but very comfortable ; and beyond these were the ballroom and the dining-hall, which was linked with my mother's suite by a long conservatory. There was a tropical heat in this passage, and I was assailed by a strong scent of lilies when I went through it. On the floor above there were several fine rooms, which were occupied by my uncle Georg who had married Princess

Marie of Greece, and my eldest uncle Nikolai Michailovich when he came out from Petersburg. Queen
Olga of Greece, consort of King Georg I and mother
to my aunt Georg, was also often there.

I myself lived with my governess in rooms beyond my
mother's suite, which were connected with the rest of the
house by a kind of covered passage. In my bedroom
there as a young girl—it sounds strange—I passed many
sleepless nights. For the so-called " white nights," which
in the Russian summer are so infinitely enchanting, were
real torture to me, because as a schoolgirl I had to go to
bed as early as half-past eight in the evening. I lay awake
for a long time in the bright room, shut in by white cur-
tains, and listened to the swallows which chased each
other round the house with long-drawn twittering—
even the birds could get no real rest in the bright
evening light ! Once a swallow even found its way into
my room. It was shortly before my engagement, and I
seized on it as a specially lucky omen :—there is a saying
that when a bird comes into a room it brings either a
happy betrothal or the blessing of children. To this day
the twittering of swallows reminds me of those summer
evenings at Michailovskoe.

I have already mentioned that my grandfather was
the youngest son of Tsar Nikolai I and the Tsarina
Charlotte, whose mother was Queen Luise. He was a tall
and commanding figure ; no one could fail to recognise
the old soldier in him. He was governor of the Caucasus for many years, and in 1887 he captured the
town of Kars. For me, his grandchild, he was always the

dearest and best grandfather that could ever exist. My childhood and the most beautiful recollections I have were influenced by this kindly man, this true nobleman : kindness and helpfulness, chivalry and tenderness were his most pronounced characteristics. I have never seen him grow angry, I have never heard him say an unkind word. He had an unqualified reverence for the majesty of the Tsar ; he never uttered a single word of criticism about him, nor would he have tolerated any such thing in his presence.

My grandfather had been brought up in the traditional close friendship with the ruling House of Prussia ; he had an enthusiastic admiration for his cousin, Kaiser Wilhelm I, and a high opinion of the Prussian army. Even in his later years, which were clouded by apoplexy and paralysis, he was as well-informed about the Prussian army as if he had been a Prussian officer, and this continued even when he had lost his memory for recent events and found difficulty in speaking. At that time friendship with Germany was still a sacred tradition, and people spoke only with admiration of Germany and its Kaiser. In regard to England one heard many words of bitter criticism, and the political friendship of Imperial Russia with Republican France at that time was still, in Court circles, regarded as something unnatural.

Unfortunately I cannot remember my grandmother, after whom I was called, for she died in 1891 when I was only four years old.

My grandfather's entourage consisted of his chamberlain, General Baranov, from the Baltic Provinces, with

147

whose cheerful and attractive daughter I struck up a close friendship, and his six adjutants, who took duty in turns. Among them were, first of all, the aged General Tolstoi, a man of small stature, very lively and very lovable, and the equally old General Winspeare, who was of Scottish origin but an Italian by birth ; he had fought at Gaeta in the King of Naples' service, and had subsequently been with my grandfather in the Turkish campaign. Of the younger members of the staff must be mentioned Prince Viasemski, Count Grabbe, who was in command of the Imperial Cossack Guard during the world war and was a member of the suite of Tsar Nikolai II at the time when he was induced to abdicate, and finally Captain Drake and Prince Chirinski. Dr. Zander, too, the medical adviser and intimate friend of the family, who spoke German like a native, was not the least important member of this circle.

The most beautiful and loyal relations existed between my grandfather and his adjutants, who had all been with him for many years, Count Tolstoi for thirty-five years. He could talk to them and they could talk to him without any formality, and he used to address them in the familiar second person. The circle into which I came was one in which there was complete loyalty, affection and respect.

For I belonged as much to this circle as to my grandfather. The members of his entourage showed me the most cordial friendship from my earliest childhood ; indeed I can say that, together with my grandfather and my uncles, they all really spoilt me. Everyone read my unspoken wishes, and they all vied with each other in making the weeks which I spent in Russia in the summer as pleasant as possible for me, especially Dr. Zander, who was particularly considerate and affectionate to me.

It was Dr. Zander, too, who practically never missed an expedition to see the sights of Petersburg or to the palaces, and carefully arranged everything for me and had me shown everything of historical interest and importance. In this way I was able to see a great deal that was worth seeing of Petersburg and its surroundings during my summer visits to Russia. Unfortunately I have never been to Moscow, for one can only form a real idea of Russia when one knows " Little Mother Moscow," the heart of Russia. But even so there was interest and excitement enough, and I want to try to describe the impressions made on me as a child and adolescent, completely unprejudiced and without the criticism of an adult mind, in the course of glorious holidays, which my relatives' affection and kindness made perfect for me.

At Michailovskoe I began the day by providing company for my grandfather while he breakfasted ; he took breakfast on one of the many terraces encircled by trees or in the oriel window of his comfortable study. From both sides of his study one could look out on the Gulf of Finland, and there were often steamers and sailing ships to be seen passing on their way from or to St. Petersburg.

Our dear friend Dr. Zander used to keep us company at breakfast ; among other duties he had to read extracts from the *Russki Invalid*, the Russian military weekly, to

my grandfather. But it was only after some years of progress in my knowledge of the Russian language that
I was able to follow what these extracts were about.
Later on, I also had to read aloud to my grandfather
during breakfast the menu for the day, which of course
was written in Russian. I had conversation lessons with
a Russian teacher, so that I was able by degrees to pierce
the mysteries of that infinitely difficult but beautiful
language. As everyone round me there spoke Russian
my ear soon got used to the sounds, a point which is of
great importance in studying a language. Unfortunately
I only carried my studies far enough to enable me to
carry on a simple conversation in Russian ; on more
difficult subjects I lacked facility in expressing my meaning, although I could understand practically all that was
said. I have retained my great liking for the musical
language of Russia, which sounds like Italian when sung,
and I only regret that after my marriage I did not carry
my studies further.

After first being with my grandfather I went to say
good morning to my mother, and then, unless I had
any lesson, I liked to pay a visit to my aunt, the Grand
Duchess Georg, and her dear little daughters or to Queen
Olga of Greece when she was staying at Michailovskoe.

Queen Olga, whose father was Admiral the Grand
Duke Konstantin, one of my grandfather's brothers,
almost made one feel that she was not of this world :
she was always kind, always ready to be helpful, and
very pious—that was her way all through her life. At
the same time she had a keen sense of humour and could

be very merry and could laugh heartily. The Russian sailors on the ships which visited Athens literally worshipped the queen like a saint ; she helped people in every walk of life ! Aunt Olga was always an intimate friend of my mother, who shared her great affection for the Russian navy, and I myself loved her like a second mother.

I last saw Aunt Olga in the spring of 1918 at Potsdam ; she had travelled on a German military train from St. Petersburg, where she had been through the early days of the revolution. As queen of an allied country she could have left Russia earlier, but she did not want to desert her relatives. Queen Victoria of Sweden gave a similar example of loyalty to her country and her family in 1918, when she was taken unawares by the revolution at Karlsruhe and stayed on for six months with her mother, the Grand Duchess Luise of Baden, although no one could have prevented her from returning to Sweden.

When Queen Olga stayed with us she was generally accompanied by her youngest son Christophoros, who was called Christo. He was quite openly his mother's favourite, but he did not show the slightest trace of being a spoilt child. He was two years younger than I was, and became my devoted friend and comrade. I used to play with him in the house or in the park, I went out with him for picnic and sight-seeing excursions, he was my companion on every interesting visit to a military display or to look over a warship, and he often helped me through my language difficulties as, like all of Queen Olga's children, he knew Russian from the time when he was quite small. In a word ours was the most beautiful and sincere friendship between young people that can possibly be imagined.

Queen Olga's mother, the Grand Duchess Alexandra Josephovna, *née* Princess of Altenburg, a sister of Queen Marie of Hanover, spent the summer at her large gothic villa at Strelna which had a wonderful park laid out in the Dutch style with islands, canals and bathing pavilions. The Grand Duchess was known within the family as Aunt Sanny. Even in her old age she was still beautiful and erect, with snow-white hair and a splendid figure. She belonged to that fine thoroughbred type which is now practically extinct : she commanded respect, but was by no means unapproachable ; she had a winning and noble disposition, she was very lovable and yet naturally reserved.

Her son lived also in Strelna—the Grand Duke Konstantin Konstantinovich, general, poet, translator, President of the Imperial Academy of Sciences ; he had been the first to translate *Hamlet* into Russian. He was fond of teasing me, and because of the height to which I had shot up he called me " Spargelgespenst " (asparagus ghost), a name which I could not shake off all through my childhood. In revenge I called his dear wife, Aunt Beth—Elissavetta Mavrikievna *née* Princess of Sachsen-Altenburg—" Great grand-aunt." We maintained very cordial family relations with their children too. Of their sons, who were all tall like their father, the third, Konstantin, fell in the war as a cavalry officer. The eldest, Johann, and two younger brothers, became victims of

DUCHESS CECILIE ON "SNOWFLAKE"

GRAND DUCHESS ANASTASIA IN HER PANHARD-LEVASSEUR, 1898

the Bolshevists ; they met a cruel death at the Alapaiev mine, where they were hurled down the shaft. My youngest uncle, Sergei, was murdered with them ; we were told that a bullet ended his life when he was being taken from the prison to the place of execution and he was thus spared the terrible death which had been intended for him.

I have already mentioned my uncle Nikolai and spoken with gratitude of the kindness and affection which he showed me. But my other uncles too, the Grand Dukes Michail, Georg, Georg Alexander and Sergei, were always so friendly and kind to me that I shall never forget them. They treated their only sister, my mother, with the greatest tenderness, and their attitude to their father was one of exemplary respect and reverence. At the same time they always expressed their opinions quite freely in his presence, even when they knew that he did not agree with them. The relations between father and children and between the children themselves were straightforward and intimate, and were genuinely patriarchal. It was, therefore, all the more heartrending for my mother to have to lose three of her dear brothers within a single year, as the result of the Russian revolution. I think she never recovered from this loss.

I am thankful that when I was young I had the privilege of experiencing in full measure how fine a thing it is when love and harmony reign within a wide family circle.

*

I must recall yet another family of friends, to meet whom was always a great joy to me. They were Princess Helene of Saxony-Altenburg and her two step-daughters Olga and Maria. Aunt Helene's mother was the clever and cultured Grand Duchess Katharina, and her father was Duke Georg of Mecklenburg-Strelitz, who entered the Russian service and, with his family, lived exclusively in Russia. Her brothers, the Dukes Georg Alexander and Karl Michail, were also Russian subjects, and in spite of their evangelical faith considered themselves to be completely Russian.

Aunt Helene had inherited her mother's gifts to a high degree ; above all she was very musical, sang beautifully and was accustomed to the society of learned and eminent people. My mother was a friend of hers and was glad that we daughters felt attracted to each other. Our friendship has been maintained up to the present day.

Princess Helene had inherited from her mother a palace on the islands near St. Petersburg, where she lived in winter, and the enchanting " Chinese Palace " at Oranienbaum which she occupied in the summer. This palace was built by Catherine II, and is probably unique in the purity of its style and the costliness of the materials of which it was constructed ; it is a veritable jewel-casket. Every summer we used to drive there once or twice, as Oranienbaum is hardly fifteen versts from Michailovskoe. We made glorious excursions into the enormous park there, which was laid out in the Dutch manner ; from the park Kronstadt with its forts and the forest of masts of the fleet at anchor could be clearly distinguished. We played all kinds of games, romped with the dogs, rode on the circular swing which itself dated from long ago, and spent many happy hours together.

In the afternoons we often took walks from Michailovskoe to the wonderful " Great Palace " of Peterhof ; it is a huge building in the baroque style, with magnificent rooms. It was here that my mother came into the world, and I shall never forget the moment when she herself led me into the room where she had been born. The castle was surrounded by the famous fountains and cascades and all kinds of fantastic statues and water-jets which in this park, as in other parks of the baroque period, visitors found so startling. What I found most attractive was a high water-pyramid, which rose in snow-white spray into the air. We generally drove to this delightful park, which extended all round the palace for a considerable distance. Then we would get out of the carriage to look at the charming little garden houses which were scattered amid woods, meadows and lakes ; in former times they were used by the imperial family for picnics and small parties. One of them, called Babignon, lay in an open position on a hill which gave it a wide view over the country ; it had been built in the last years of the reign of Tsar Nikolai I in the Pompeian style, with painted frescos. A small country-house, " Monplaisir," had been built by Peter the Great in the Dutch style, and was decorated with beautiful pictures. Another pavilion lay on a small island in the middle of an artificial lake, and could only be reached by means of a miniature ferry-boat. Other villas lay hidden among the trees of the park. The so-called Roman Baths at Potsdam, and perhaps also Charlottenhof, are reminiscent of those exquisite little buildings which in some cases date back to Catherine the Great.

When I looked at them I would give my fantasy full play, and would see in imagination, in the liveliest colours, the ladies of Catherine's Court in hooped petticoats and high wigs dancing their minuets or listening to a concert of flutes in the lofty mirrored halls. I also liked to picture to myself the generation of the period of Alexander I or Tsar Nikolai I and Tsarina Charlotte, both when I was on those merry outings and when I met the people of the Court.

One evening each week there was a concert in the park at Peterhof, given by the imperial orchestra, who were called "the Reds" from the colour of their uniform. It was an orchestra of selected musicians, and it played with remarkable brilliance. Now and then my mother would release me from going to bed at the regulation early hour and take me with her to Peterhof for the evening concert. We would stroll slowly round the music pavilion or along the neighbouring paths within hearing distance.

I remember quite distinctly that on one such occasion a selection from the Bizet opera *Arlésienne* gave me particular pleasure, and a charming Paderewski minuet went on running in my head for a long time afterwards. I bought both pieces arranged for the piano so that I could play them at home and continue to enjoy them. To my joy, the orchestra also played selections from the Wagner operas, and there was always some classical music which it played to perfection.

At an earlier period and even in the first years of the reign of Tsar Nikolai II these evening concerts had been an outstanding social event. The imperial family had then generally driven to the concert in the long "Linieke" coaches, of which, as already mentioned, we also had a specimen at Schwerin. But by my time all of that belonged to the remote past.

*

When we went to Petersburg we used either the railway from Strelna or a lovely steamer, which always lay in readiness for the imperial household to make the crossing from Peterhof through Kronstadt Bay. On the sea route we saw on our right the bare Russian coast and on our left the wooded shores of Finland, which recall the Frische Haff near Königsberg.

A carriage was waiting for us on our arrival, and we began our drive round the town, which on the whole did not make any very favourable impression on me. For all its unique features, the town can hardly be called beautiful. The Neva with its wide quay and the many palaces on its banks was the only magnificent view; it was especially fine looking down from the Winter Palace on the pointed tower of the Peter-and-Paul Church and the Admiralty with the tall pillars in front of it. I was standing on the very scene of all those historical events of which I had heard and read so much, magnificent pageants and terrible disasters ! Then and afterwards my imagination was busy with the historic dramas which had been played there, to the weal or woe of Russia ! And in its present, as in its past, the town showed the sharpest contrast. Nowhere else could one see luxurious splendour so close to the most bitter poverty : men and women in rags among the carriages of the rich, and miserable wretches among elegant officers and uniformed officials. Here was the visible clash of Western civilisation with the primitive life of Asia.

On the Nevski Prospekt we looked at the peculiar Gosting-Dvor, a great covered market painted white, which was over a hundred years old and contained arcades with a great many shops which were not exactly elegant. At other shops we bought the characteristically Russian lacquered boxes or pretty little wooden objects. In the lovely jewellery shops we saw the most enchanting enamelled work, which was very popular as presents at the Russian Court and in the family.

Among the sights of Petersburg the Winter Palace has remained most vivid in my mind, a gigantic sprawling structure in white and red. It looked as if the people of the grey North had tried to conjure up the gay colours of the South.

Within the Winter Palace the rooms of the various generations of rulers had as a rule been kept in their original state, so that one could get an accurate idea of how the individual Tsars and Tsarinas had lived. The rooms which interested me most were those of my great-grandmother, the Tsarina Alexandra Feodorovna (Charlotte of Prussia), and of the Tsarina Elizabeth, Alexander I's consort, of whom I had heard a great deal from my uncle Nikolai. In the study of Alexander II I saw the camp-bed on which the Tsar had bled to death after the terrible outrage in which both his legs were blown off. In the Jewel Chamber I saw the gorgeous Crown insignia, especially the Byzantine crown and the sceptre with the famous Orlov diamond ; and I saw also the ghostly wax statue of Peter the Great and innumerable paintings, mostly of battles, in countless halls of gigantic proportions. But I can hardly recollect the artistic treasures of the famous Hermitage ; as a child I was most interested in the many mementos, both of historical and personal significance, of my ancestors.

Unfortunately, too, I only knew my grandfather's palace through these short visits, and I never stayed in it. I remember particularly the apartments of my uncle Nikolai, as they were full of objects of historical interest. One charming picture of the Tsarina Elizabeth evoked my greatest admiration. Since the revolution I have often wondered where this picture is now.

The Grand Duke Alexei, who has already been mentioned, lived in a wonderfully pretty little palace with a large garden on the Neva ; he often invited my mother and me to lunch with him there. At the gate there was a double watch of sailors of the Naval Guard, a crack corps whose Commander-in-Chief was the Dowager Tsarina Maria Feodorovna ; as a special mark of distinction they wore on their caps the St. George ribbon, which was the ribbon of the highest military order in Russia. Both officers and men were always favoured by the imperial family, and they were very much pampered. In 1917 a company of the Naval Guard was on duty with the Tsarina at Tsarskoe Selo—and shortly after the revolution had been proclaimed it went over to the Reds ! This was one of the first and most bitter disillusionments which the Tsar and his family were to experience in those terrible days.

I was last in the Grand Duke Alexei's palace in 1911, when the German Embassy was rebuilt and the Palace was taken over by them during the rebuilding. Count and Countess Pourtalès on that occasion gave a dinner for the Crown Prince and myself, which was followed by a reception. It made me feel quite strange to visit this house again after so many years and in such altered circumstances.

But it would take me too far afield if I tried to recount everything I saw in the way of palaces, memorials, parks, and other sights. It is enough to say that I always returned from St. Petersburg to Michailovskoe filled with the most vivid impressions of the signs of a great past which was closely associated with myself.

*

How care-free we all were at that time, how brimming over with the happiness of youth ! We used to have joint dancing lessons, held alternately in one house after another ; once it would be at Strelna, then at Snamenskaia, and on a third occasion at our own place Michailovskoe.

Our dancing master was an instructor from the Imperial Russian Ballet, who wore long side-whiskers and in spite of his advanced years was still extraordinarily graceful. He explained everything in French and himself went through the necessary " pas " in front of us, and we followed him with more or less accomplished grace. Besides the mazurka, the chaconne and the polka-mazurka were at that time the favourite dances in Russia.

And it was in the pretty ball-room at Michailovskoe that I attended my first ball ! I looked forward to it with great pleasure, and my excitement over this event of my girlhood was equally great.

Many of our relatives and a number of the young members of the Court circle, as well as some of the officers of the *Svietlana* whom we knew, took part in this festivity. Thanks to the dancing lessons I was expert in the various dances which were then in fashion, and so I was lucky enough to find many partners.

The climax of the festivities was the mazurka, a kind of cotillon, which concluded the ball. It was led by an officer of the Tsarina's Lancers from Peterhof, who danced with great animation. The ladies danced and moved forward in the mazurka-step, each holding her partner's hand, while the men had to perform special steps, rattling their spurs and striking their heels on the ground. This gave the dance, which whirled through the hall at a furiously rapid tempo, its peculiar rhythm. The Slavonic temperament as well as the musical and rhythmical feeling of the Russians is most vigorously expressed in the mazurka, and I have always been sorry that this was the only occasion on which I have danced in a real mazurka.

The ball was a great success and my good comrade Christo and I performed wonders during the intervals at the heavily-laden buffet and amused ourselves gloriously, and for a long time afterwards we enjoyed talking about that lovely evening. My dear kind grandfather looked on, enjoying my unconcealed pleasure, and talked with the guests in his courteous, friendly way.

CHAPTER VIII

AT THE COURT OF THE TSAR

Even in my time the family of the Tsar lived in almost complete retirement. Already a heavy sense of oppression prevailed at the Imperial Court ; it was as if everyone were always waiting for something terrible to happen. Since the horrible murder of Tsar Alexander II and the railway outrage against Tsar Alexander III, everyone was prepared for a catastrophe at any moment, and every moment expecting an attempt at assassination. To live in small houses, in confined rooms under a strong guard still seemed to offer a certain security. But it was an existence that was almost like imprisonment.

It seemed to me that the life of those dear people was hardly worth living, and I often wondered if it would not have been better to move more freely among the people and to appear more in public, rather than to live like that behind walls and military cordons. There is probably a good deal of truth in the belief that fear of a danger increases it, but that fearlessness can overcome and indeed do away with dangers. The tragedy of the Russian imperial family has only confirmed my belief in this law of nature.

The forces which are involved in Russia are firmly rooted in the fundamental nature of the people, and in their historical development, and have therefore become

163

so powerful that it is scarcely possible for a single individual to control them. Rulers like Alexander I and Nikolai I, however, mastered these dark forces, and nothing happened to them. A dominating personality will always know how to win through.

I had the opportunity of getting to know the Tsar and Tsarina, not only on official occasions, but also in the intimacy of the family circle. This was the case especially during the visits which my mother always asked permission to make immediately after our arrival. Sometimes the visit was postponed for several days, because the Tsarina Alexandra Feodorovna, who was then generally known as " the young Tsarina " to distinguish her from the Dowager Tsarina, was often ill. Then we were generally invited to a family lunch in their most intimate circle. Their Majesties did not occupy any of the magnificent palaces of Peterhof, but had a small, almost commonplace villa built for them in the Alexandria Park near the sea. Everything was on a miniature scale, but this just suited these two people who loved simplicity and would have liked best to live entirely for each other and their children.

Tsar Nikolai was an extraordinarily kind host. There was something specially friendly in his look and manner ; his shining eyes with their benevolent expression were absolutely fascinating. He always looked directly and searchingly at the person he was talking to, and yet at the same time gently and kindly. He gave the impression of a noble and sincere character, and I am convinced that he desired nothing but good. But he had not enough strength of will, and it was a fatality that this man should occupy the throne of Russia just at this time. His father would probably have been better fitted to deal with the vast problems that confronted Russia at the beginning of the twentieth century.

The Tsarina was very beautiful to look at. Her regular features and delicate mouth, drooping a little at the corners, gave her face an expression of fatalistic melancholy—even then I was conscious of this impression. She was very attractive but very reserved, and suffered from nervousness which was almost a disease. If a stranger was presented to her, her face flushed a deep red and she could hardly find a word to say to the person who stood before her. She was never popular in Russia, and suffered greatly from the fact that the Dowager Tsarina was a much greater favourite. But in the family circle the Tsarina could be very merry. She was a loving mother, an exemplary wife. The marriage of these two hapless people was a unique spiritual harmony, and it seems to me that this boundless happiness in their married life was a compensation for the bitter sufferings which they had to endure.

Their little daughters were the most delightful children. We often met them on an outing in one of the beautiful parks. They used to drive with their nurse in an open landau ; they were sweet creatures with long fair hair and blue eyes gazing round contentedly.

Our visits were returned by Their Majesties at Michailovskoe, and naturally there was always considerable excitement when word spread that the " Gosudar "

(Ruler) was on his way. When both the Tsar and Tsarina came they used a victoria drawn by magnificent Orloff trotters and driven by a particularly fat coachman (the fatter he was, the more imposing !). When the Tsar came by himself he drove in quite an unpretentious one-horse carriage, called a " Droshky."

The coachmen wore Russian dress, that is, a dark-green caftan with a brightly-coloured border round the neck and an embroidered belt under which the coat lay in a number of padded folds, and on their heads a wide lacquered hat with a black wig attached to it. They held their arms stretched straight out in front of them with one rein in each hand. But it looked splendid, and I liked it tremendously. The coachmen and footmen of the imperial household wore braided livery and three-cornered hats.

The Tsar was always escorted by a single mounted Cossack—but of course a particularly dependable one ; even when he went out for a ride he never had a larger retinue with him. At every crossroads, however, there were men whom it was not difficult to recognise as detectives in spite of their civilian clothes ; they were keeping the closest possible watch along the route. Soldiers were posted round the Alexandria Park in such positions that they were in sight of each other, and it was the same on every section of the railway along which the imperial train ran.

*

The Dowager Tsarina Maria Feodorovna. lived in the so-called Cottage of Alexandria, the park of which bounded the eastern side of the great park of Peterhof. It was a comfortable house which had once been presented to the Tsarina Alexandra Feodorovna (Charlotte of Prussia) by her imperial consort and had been her favourite residence. The rooms were not high, and the whole setting was old-fashioned and comfortable. There were green plants everywhere, in the corners and behind sofas, and on the table a mass of nick-nacks, which reminded me of my great-grandmother Alexandrine's apartments—which was not strange, seeing that the former owner of these trinkets was my great-grandmother's sister ! A steep flight of iron steps led to the upper storey, where the Dowager Tsarina's pretty boudoir, the only modern room, was situated ; it was long and narrow, but very cosy. The walls were panelled with Karelian birch, and the deep sofas and chairs were covered with flowered cretonnes. Water-colours hung on the walls, and there were also innumerable family portraits ; precious little hand-bells, ashtrays and other attractive Russian products which were then fashionable lay on small tables.

I always very much liked visiting the Tsarina Maria Feodorovna, who was generally called " Aunt Minny " in the family ; for there was something very charming in her gestures, her deep, slightly husky voice, and particularly her marvellously beautiful and expressive eyes. She was very short, but her bearing, her distinguished and forceful personality, and the intelligence which shone in her face, made her the perfect figure of a queen. Wherever she went, her winning smile conquered the hearts of the people. The way in which she bowed when passing in her carriage was charming in its gracefulness. She was extraordinarily well loved in Russia, and everyone had confidence in her. Everywhere she was the central figure, within the family and in Court society, and it was characteristic of her that she was most intimate with those who had the highest appreciation of sympathy and generosity. She was a faithful and devoted Patroness of the many benevolent institutions in which she was interested, and a real mother to her people. I am not in a position to say anything of her political views, and I therefore refrain from expressing any opinion in this connection. To me she was always uniformly friendly and kind, and I always greatly respected and admired her.

The little family festivals which we celebrated with the Dowager Tsarina at Alexandria, as for example her name-days, have always been among my most cherished recollections. After a Te Deum, which was sung in the little chapel, we used to meet in the garden, where a cheerful meal was served ; the young people were left to themselves, and amused each other with games and conversation. We spent many delightful evenings too with Aunt Minny and our other relatives in the family circle, during those summers with their long light nights. Among our kinsfolk was the Grand Duke Michail, her youngest son, who used to come over from Gatschina where he was stationed, and added to the general gaiety.

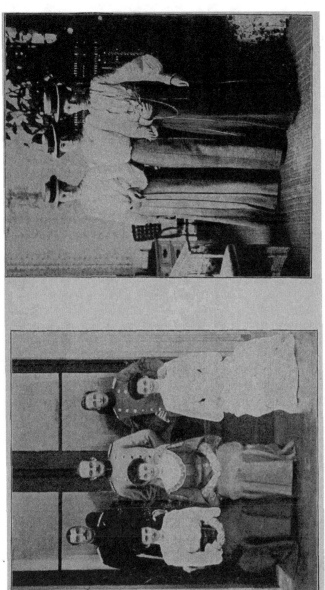

PRINCE CHRISTIAN AND PRINCESS ALEXANDRINE OF
DENMARK; GRAND DUKE FRIEDRICH FRANZ IV AND
GRAND DUCHESS ALEXANDRA; CROWN PRINCE WILHELM
AND DUCHESS CECILIE IN THE AUTUMN OF 1904

GRAND DUCHESS ANASTASIA WITH HER TWO
DAUGHTERS, ALEXANDRINE AND CECILIE

We were very much attached to Xenia and Olga, the daughter of the Dowager Tsarina, whom we often met at her house. The Grand Duchess Xenia had married my uncle Alexander, and lived with him and her seven charming children at the " Farm," a little house not far from the Dowager Tsarina's " Alexandria," which had formerly been the favourite abode of Tsar Alexander II. One of their daughters was the lovely Princess Irina, who later on married Prince Felix Yussupov, well-known in connection with the murder of Rasputin.

If time allowed we used to pay a number of other ceremonial visits to Grand Duchesses and aunts. My mother attached great importance to courteous formalities, particularly in relation to older people ; I have always tried to observe them, even if it is often inconvenient, and perhaps no longer seems to suit the times in which we live.

*

I have an unforgettable vision of the sister of the Tsarina, wife of the Grand Duke Sergius : Elisaveta Feodorovna, *née* Princess Elisabeth of Hessen-Darmstadt. It was at the christening of the heir to the throne, at which I was present. After standing continuously for some time in the church I began to feel rather faint, as I always did, and one of my dear uncles took me into another part of the building, where I could sit down and recover a little. As we were going back into the chapel the Grand Duchess came towards us, in Russian dress with magnificent emerald ornaments. In that dress, and in the setting which surrounded her, at that moment she seemed, in the radiance of her beauty, like some ikon, some old Byzantine saint which had come to life !

How often I have seen this picture in my mind's eye, how vividly it came back to me when I heard the news of her martyr's death in the shaft of the mine at Alapaiev.

At the time when I saw her she was not yet a widow. A year after her husband, the Grand Duke Sergius, was blown to pieces in front of the Kremlin in Moscow by a bomb thrown by an anarchist. When the Grand Duchess rushed out of the Kremlin after the fearful explosion she found only the shattered body of her husband. She insisted on visiting the murderer in his prison cell, in order to ask him why he had destroyed her life's happiness and to save his soul by means of religious exhortation. But he would not let anything lead him astray from his anarchist principles, although he was moved by the noble bearing of the widow of his victim, and the sensational interview passed without visible result.

After this terrible event the Grand Duchess devoted her life entirely to charitable objects. She founded the Martha and Mary Convent of sisters of mercy in Moscow, became its abbess and wore nun's dress, without actually becoming a nun. Like the Tsarina she was inclined to mysticism in her religious views. But in politics she had considerably more insight than her sister, and it is said that the Grand Duchess raised her voice in warning when events during the world war became more and more unfavourable to the monarchy.

The fact that the Bolshevists laid violent hands on the life of this pious and charitable woman must fill everyone with horror. She was thrown into the prison at Alapaiev with some of her relatives, and was voluntarily accompanied by two of the ladies from her convent. Only one of them yielded to her entreaty that they should leave her and retrieve their freedom ; the other went with her mistress to death.

A pious monk took her body and her companion's right across Siberia, under conditions of the greatest difficulty and self-sacrifice, and brought them at last to Jerusalem, where they now rest near the Church of the Sepulchre. God alone knows why He makes his chosen ones drink the cup of suffering to the dregs.

*

But let us turn away from these terrible scenes, back to the time of my youth, which was still able to witness the full glory of the Court of the Romanovs !

During the seven summer visits which I spent in Russia one after the other, I had the opportunity of sharing in a number of important Court festivities : the wedding of my cousin, the Grand Duchess Helene Vladimirovna with Prince Nicholas of Greece, the christening of the youngest daughter of the Tsar and Tsarina, and finally the christening of the little Grand Duke who was heir to the throne.

The wedding took place at the great Palace of Tsarskoe Selo, to which we drove in a troika early in the morning. All the Grand Duchesses and their ladies came in Russian dress and wearing the " kokoshnik " ; this was an oval head-dress covered with silk and ornamented with diamonds or pearls. In the case of the Tsarina's it was a diadem of diamonds, made in the prescribed form. The " kokoshnik " might only be worn by Russian Grand Duchesses and ladies of the Court. The dresses of the Grand Duchesses were entirely of white satin, cut on the lines of a caftan with a close-fitting bodice on the front of which was a jewelled band ; the dresses had small puffed sleeves and long trains of coloured velvet from the waist. Each lady-in-waiting wore the colours of her mistress. The foreign Princesses appeared *en grande toilette* with trains of the usual pattern, and the so-called Court décolletage, leaving the shoulders bare, which was also the rule in Berlin.

As I was not yet grown-up, and therefore not subject to the strict rules of Court etiquette, my mother had had a Russian fancy-dress made for me. It consisted of a pink silk caftan, cut in the style of a Russian court-dress with long sleeves of gathered chiffon. The front was crossed by the usual band, on which (imitation) pearls were sewn. My hair was plaited in two thick plaits bound with strings of pearls, and on my head I wore a small " kokoshnik." In this costume I naturally thought I looked very striking.

In the Great Palace the very lengthy wedding ceremony took place first, in which crowns were held above the heads of the bridal pair by the young men of the family, including my brother. In front of the altar lay a strip of white satin. It was an old superstition that whichever of the bridal pair first trod on this piece of silk, which was supposed to represent their life's course, would be the dominant partner in the marriage, that is would " rule the roost."

After the wedding they went to the banqueting hall through the long corridors and halls between double lines formed by the members of the royal household ; right and left stood the numerous ladies and gentlemen who held appointments at Court and others who moved in Court circles, the gentlemen in their brilliant uniforms and glittering decorations, the ladies in full dress and wearing costly jewels—a scene of magnificent colour. This was called the " Vikhod " (la sortie) but I have never been able to discover the exact meaning of this designation. Probably it had been so called since the time of Catherine the Great. The banquet, too, lasted an interminably long time. After it was over came the so-called polonaise, the counterpart of our torch-dance, but without the torches. The couples kept on changing their partners, and meanwhile they moved forward, one behind the other, between bowing courtiers. The bands played the beautiful polonaises of Glinka and Tchaikovski.

At this point, however, inexorable fate stepped in : the time had come for a schoolgirl to go home ! On this matter my mother knew no mercy. When she had decided how long I might stay at a function of that kind not even the most beseeching entreaties could move her, whether mine or my uncle's, though the latter pleaded vehemently that I should be allowed to stay on. To-day

I admire her firmness. I am afraid that I am not anything like so firm with my children.

With heavy heart, therefore, I had to leave my partner, and was accompanied by a gentleman-in-waiting to our apartments, which I found that my governess had already reached. Then regretfully I took off the beautiful dress in which I would never see myself again, and in a moment I was sitting in the troika, which brought us at a swift pace back to Michailovskoe. The drive was some slight recompense for the pleasures I was missing, as a troika was even at that time a novelty, and the rapid drive with the three horses, two of which galloped at the sides while the horse in the centre kept to an even trot, was extremely original and interesting to me.

The two christening ceremonies which were celebrated at the Palace in Peterhof were similar to the wedding, but without the polonaise afterwards. The child who was to be christened was driven from the Tsar's small villa to the great Palace in Peterhof in a state carriage drawn by six white horses, escorted by two squadrons of the Horse Guards; the stately head of the Tsarina's household, Princess Galitsin, held the child in her arms. On arrival at the palace they moved *en grand cortège* to the chapel, and the infant, in a long ceremony, was received into the bosom of the Orthodox Church through holy baptism. After the church ceremony there was again a procession through the long galleries, flanked to right and left by the ladies and gentlemen of the Imperial Court, and then a great banquet followed.

The christening of the unfortunate heir to the throne

was conducted in the same way, and also at Peterhof, although it should really have taken place in the capital and with the very utmost magnificence. But the practice of avoiding St. Petersburg for all great festivals had become already so established that even on this occasion no departure from it was made.

*

A visit made by my mother and myself to my uncle Sergei when he was in camp left very pleasant memories in my mind. The manœuvres were in progress, and the troops were quartered in a village. The choir of my uncle's battery sang Russian soldier-songs and folk-songs which were mostly in a melancholy minor key and so closely expressed the spirit of the Russian people. To suffer, suffer, and go on suffering—that seems to be the fate of this good-natured pious people. At sunset the retreat was sounded, and a tattoo accompanied the evening prayer.

The finest military displays at which I have been present were two parades in the camp at Krasnoe Selo, one of which was held in honour of the Shah of Persia.

On the preceding evening we went to the camp in the imperial train with the whole of the Tsar's family, and then we passed in a ceremonial procession along the lanes of the camp—the Tsarina with us and the Grand Duchesses in carriages harnessed à la Daumont, and the Tsar with the Grand Dukes on horseback. The troops, consisting of the Guard and regiments from the interior of Russia, were drawn up in double line, and as the Tsar approached broke into repeated long-drawn cheers, which, compared with our short military " Hurrah ! ", produced a melancholy, wailing effect.

A tent had been pitched on rising ground beyond the camp. There we alighted, and listened to a military concert which now began, while the officers were presented to Their Majesties, and regimental reports and announcements were made. The scene presented by the assembled company was an extremely gay one : the men all in their brilliant uniforms, the ladies in white or light-coloured dresses with the large picture-hats which were then the fashion, and carrying beautiful lace sunshades. Just before sunset the ceremonial evening tattoo sounded and the evening service was recited, just as I had heard it on board ship.

In the evening there was a performance in the little camp theatre in which the imperial corps de ballet and dramatic company from Petersburg took part. Next morning we drove out to the parade on the great parade-ground where the troops drilled in the summer. All the ladies, with the exception of the two Tsarinas, had seats in a gigantic tent from which the whole ground could be seen. The regiments were already lined up for the parade. First the Tsar rode down the lines, beside the Daumont carriage drawn by white horses in which his mother and his wife were seated, and immediately behind him came two trumpeters. Then followed in procession the Grand Dukes and generals in command. After this the Tsarinas joined us in our tent. The Tsar pulled up in front of

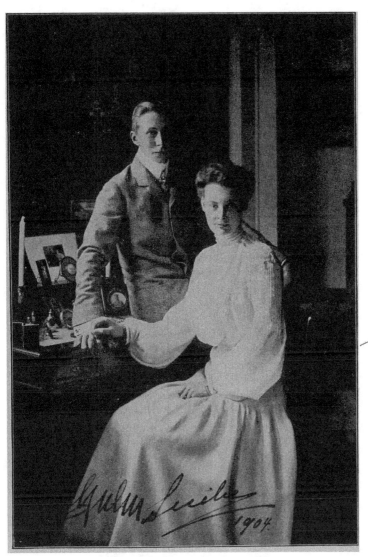

THE BETROTHED COUPLE, 1904

them, attended by only the two staff trumpeters, while the troops marched past.

It was an amazingly beautiful sight. The magnificent horse-guard regiments rode at the head, the gay hussars followed, the light lancers, then the countless lines of infantry, guards, riflemen, sappers, artillery, and finally the Cossacks, who found it difficult to hold in their foaming steeds. The troops were in marching kit, with blouse and cap, as it was summer.

The Tsar himself gave the orders for the cavalry and artillery, and the two trumpeters transmitted his commands—" March ! " " Trot ! " " Gallop ! " —by means of ringing trumpet calls.

After a second march-past in different formation the parade was concluded, and the Tsar joined us in the tent. His eyes shone even more brilliantly than was their wont, and he seemed to be carried away by the happiness of being among his troops. In those days they were still loyal to their " Gosudar-Imperator."

These parades left an indelible impression on my mind. It was with great emotion and pleasure that after the war I read the faithful and inspiring description given by Krasnov in his book *From the Imperial Eagle to the Red Flag*.

CHAPTER IX

JOURNEYS WITH MY GRANDFATHER

During our summer stay at Michailovskoe in 1903 there occurred an event which was to make a serious change in my life : the severe illness of my dear grandfather. In the second half of August two warships were to be launched at St. Petersburg, and we intended to be there for the ceremony with the whole of the imperial family. We all looked forward to it with pleasure, especially I myself, as I had never been present at the launch of a ship.

On the evening before the launch my grandfather was playing billiards with his sons as usual. When I said good-night to him he was standing as erect as ever, with his cue in his hand, and tenderly and affectionately kissed me good-night. I went to bed happy and looking forward to the morrow, when we were to make an early start.

But next morning I was awakened with the terrible news that during the night my grandfather had had a stroke, and that the whole of his right side was paralysed and his speech too had been affected and was indistinct.

Our participation in the launching ceremony was at once abandoned, and we passed the day in great anxiety. We felt more relieved when my grandfather's condition got no worse, and after a few days he was out of danger and he even partly recovered his speech. But all the same it was very hard for us all to see our beloved grandfather paralysed and confined to his chair.

All plans were now altered. First we stayed longer than usual at Michailovskoe, but there could no longer be any talk of my making my début that winter in St. Petersburg, as my mother had originally intended, because my grandfather was ordered to stay in the south. My mother had therefore to travel earlier than usual to Cannes to get everything ready, and in October my grandfather followed in a special train.

In spite of our anxiety for my grandfather these autumn weeks at Michailovskoe had their pleasant side, for now that the many functions were over life within the family was more intimate and peaceful ; and out of doors it was fascinating to watch the leaves gradually changing colour in the beautiful parks. Now that the summer population had departed these parks were empty and on our walks and drives seemed to belong to us alone.

Autumn set in particularly early in Russia that year. The avenues of trees gave an impression of inexpressible melancholy, with their leaves fluttering slowly down into the canals and pools and forming yellow and brown spots of colour on the unruffled surface of the water. The great ebb of Nature's life produced an even more moving impression in the vast Russian landscape than with us in Germany.

Looking back to-day I think of these autumn days as

symbolic of the great suffering and death which not long after descended on this vast Empire : death on a scale which the world has probably never seen before, and suffering such as a people can hardly ever have known, a catastrophe in which everything, yes, everything which culture, morals and faith had built up during centuries of development, was to be destroyed. How great is God's mercy, that he does not let us look into the future !

Russia, with all its associations of my childhood, was something great and beautiful, something of quite special significance in my life. The recollection of all the beautiful things I experienced there, all the kindness shown me by people who were dear to me, will live for ever in my heart.

The terrible catastrophe of the revolution has destroyed the Russia which I knew and loved, and cast it into the darkest depths of an abyss from which it will hardly be able to raise itself again within any period that can be conceived by human beings. In sorrow and resignation to God's inscrutable will I stand before an event which can scarcely find its parallel in the history of the world.

Only memory still preserves the image of men whose life has long since passed away, but whose deeds are written in the " Book of Life," hereafter, judged by God's righteousness, to live on in transfigured form in the Kingdom of God.

*

In the course of November I left my home at Mecklenburg and travelled to Cannes. My grandfather had already settled down in a beautiful and spacious villa near Villa Wenden. He was visibly improving in health in the mild climate, and often went out for drives, but his legs remained as before almost completely paralysed, and it was only with a great effort that he was able, supported by two attendants, to walk a few steps in his room.

I tried as far as I could to help in looking after him and entertaining him. At first I visited him twice a day, and tried to keep him amused by recounting my little adventures. When he got stronger in the course of the winter I used to lunch with him every day, sometimes by myself and sometimes with my mother or one of my uncles, who took it in turns during the winter to stay with him at Cannes. In the evening I would pay him a second visit, which I could see pleased him. His touching affection for me and the expression of happiness which always lighted up his dear face when I arrived, richly repaid me for any discomfort which being tied to these regular sick-visits might have caused me as a child who liked activity.

That winter the political situation in the Far East had become acute. In the middle of negotiations between the Cabinets in February, 1904, Japanese torpedo-boats, without any previous declaration of war, suddenly attacked the Russian squadron in the outer roads of Port Arthur, and damaged three ships. That was the beginning of that disastrous war which brought Russia defeat after defeat and finally the first revolution. I still re-member quite distinctly the impression made on my youthful mind when the news came of the attack and the subsequent declaration of war.

I recall particularly a visit which we made to a con-valescent home which was filled with Russian officers. They belonged to ships which had made a sortie from Port Arthur and taken refuge in a neutral port. The ships were disarmed and the wounded officers brought on a neutral ship to the south of France. When we visited them the following winter, the officers confirmed the terrible descriptions of the battle which we had read in the French newspapers. As the naval battles at Port Arthur were the first battles which had been fought with modern guns and munitions, and the effect on the ships had been devastating beyond anything that could pre-viously have been imagined, the description of it produced a very deep impression.

I remember too that I provided myself with an album into which I pasted cuttings from the papers and pictures of the Russo-Japanese theatre of war, which is an indi-cation of how actively my childish imagination occupied itself with the war, of which we naturally heard a great deal through my mother's Russian relatives and ac-quaintances. In another chapter I shall mention other experiences which had a connection with the Russo-Japanese war.

In the spring Grandpapa was brought first to Baden-Baden on his way north, and to my great delight I was allowed to travel with him. We left Cannes only in the middle of May and thus for once experienced the really hot and marvellous spring which we missed when we made our departure as usual on May 1st.

On the day before our departure, when I was sitting with my mother in the smoking-room having tea, and we looked out through the wide-open glass doors on the magnificent panorama below us, we decided that the following year also we should give ourselves this pleasure and stay at Cannes again until this date. But in the following year quite a different thing happened : I left Cannes earlier instead of later, because my wedding was imminent !

So in the middle of May we travelled in a special train to Baden-Baden. It was astonishing how my grandfather grew more and more interested and vigorous in the course of the journey. When, on our arrival at the station of Baden-Oos, the station-master came to see him in his carriage, my grandfather was already able to talk with him almost as well as in the days when he had been quite well. He enquired whether the members of the family of the Grand-Ducal House were in Baden-Baden, and showed a keen interest in everything that had happened in this dear little town during the past year.

. At Baden-Baden we took up our residence in a villa attached to the Hôtel Stephanie ; Grandpapa occupied the lower floor, and I and Miss King had the front rooms of the upper floor, looking out on the Oos and the gardens.

It made my grandfather very happy to see once more

the familiar squares and streets of this charming water-ing-place. He received frequent visits, too, from his Baden relatives as well as from many Russian and German friends and acquaintances. As time went on he recovered the use of his legs to such an extent that, leaning on his attendant and a stout stick, he was able to undertake short walks in the gardens. He liked very much to sit on a bench and look at the visitors taking their promenade, and they would give him a respectful greeting. As a rule one of his adjutants or Dr. Zander would accompany us on these walks. Occasionally he invited guests to lunch and now and then there would be an excursion into the glorious country round Baden-Baden, which, with its dense woods, its green slopes and its trees in blossom is like a fairyland in the spring.

Of his Baden relatives who used to visit Grandpapa he probably liked best to see his brother-in-law; the Grand Duke Friedrich I, and the Grand Duchess Luise, besides their two daughters, Queen Victoria of Sweden and Princess Wilhelm of Baden, *née* Princess Leuchten-berg.

The Grand Duke was an exceptionally friendly and dignified old gentleman, who was sincerely respected and loved by the people of his country. As he was the old Kaiser's son-in-law and himself an outstanding person-ality he had on several occasions played a part in the politics of the German Empire. Grand Duchess Luise was an ideal sovereign. She had inherited from her mother, the Kaiserin Augusta, the unswerving sense of

ENTRY OF THE DUCHESS CECILIE INTO BERLIN

duty which she showed towards her country. She founded a number of benevolent institutions and directed them in an exemplary way. She never wearied of visiting these institutions or fulfilling the many other duties of a sovereign princess. Even when she was quite old she never gave herself any rest. She was either on a round of visits to hospitals, educational institutes, cookery schools or other institutions, or she was receiving people with whom she discussed everything in every detail and from whom she got reports on everything ; and she showed her warm sympathy even in purely personal matters. I had the impression that she knew practically every inhabitant of Baden. When during the war I walked through any hospital in Berlin or elsewhere and came across some wounded soldier from Baden, he was sure to know his Grand Duchess personally.

What bitter tragedy there was in the fact that, at the conclusion of the war and at the beginning of the revolution, the warm-hearted Grand Duchess of Baden was abused as " the Prussian woman " and insulted in the most ungrateful way in her own country ! But fortunately this attitude by degrees gave place to a juster view, so that the Grand Duchess Luise was allowed to spend the evening of her life peacefully at Baden Castle. And when she died the great sympathy shown by the population was a clear indication of the loyalty and affection for her which still survived among her people. In the Prussian royal family, too, the position of the Grand Duchess Luise was one which always commanded great respect. As the only daughter of Kaiser

Wilhelm I and Kaiserin Augusta she faithfully preserved their traditions, which when I married were still in every respect authoritative, both at the Prussian Court and in family affairs. Grand Duchess Luise was present at all family festivals celebrated in Berlin. On such occasions she always occupied the room which she had had as a girl, in the right wing on the ground floor of the old Kaiser's Palace. There she met her parents' faithful friends and many other acquaintances who shared her conception of the duties of life.

The Grand Duchess showed a particularly sympathetic interest in the institutions which had once been founded and cared for by her mother. Not a Sunday passed without her sending a lengthy letter of greetings to the Principal of the Augusta Hospital in Berlin. And when she stayed in Berlin or Potsdam she never failed to visit this hospital and the Augusta Institute at Potsdam, and to have long and detailed talks with the Principals, sisters, instructresses and the patients or children. She knew the sisters and their charges quite intimately.

I took a special interest in the Grand Duchess because of my double relationship with her. Especially after the death of my mother-in-law, the Kaiserin, my great-aunt showed me infinite sympathy, particularly in her understanding of the need to carry on the Kaiserin's work in the sphere of social welfare. To me it was really like a consecration when the aged patriarch of the House, on my last visit to Baden-Baden, blessed me with her advice and encouragement on the many responsible tasks which lay before me.

In 1904 both the Grand Duke and the Grand Duchess were still very active and in full possession of their vigour, even though the Grand Duke was already quite advanced in years. He was six years older than my grandfather. My grandmother Olga had been his very much younger sister.

My grandfather had a particular affection for his niece, daughter of the Grand Duke and Grand Duchess, the late Queen Victoria of Sweden, who was then Crown Princess. I shared to the full this affection for the Queen. Her noble disposition and lofty outlook on life have always served as an example to me. Crown Prince Gustav, the present King, was also at Baden-Baden at that time and always showed me great cordiality, so that my stay in that beautiful spot was made even more pleasant by these family associations.

In this circle, too, I often heard them talk of by-gone generations, which aroused my keen interest. My great-aunt could tell stories of her childhood about the Grand Duchess Stephanie, who was the niece of Napoleon and Josephine. In spite of her French origin it would appear that her outlook was completely German. The unfortunate woman had lost her sons at an early age, and it was said that they had not died a natural death. Grand Duchess Luise also pointed out to me the portraits at Castle Baden of the Baden princesses, daughters of the Hereditary Prince Karl Ludwig and grand-daughters of the so-called " Great Land-gravine " of Hessen ; they were the Tsarina Elizabeth of Russia, Queen Karoline of Bavaria, and Queen

Friederike of Sweden, wife of the deposed monarch Gustav Adolf IV.

Another guest whom we were always glad to see was Princess Wilhelm of Baden, Grandpapa's niece and mother of Prince Max. She inherited her fine profile from her grandfather Tsar Nikolai I—her maiden name was Princess Marie Romanovsky, Duchess of Leuchtenberg ; she was very straightforward and sincere in everything she did and said. She was always dressed in a man's style, that is, a jacket with a waistcoat and tie, which gave her rather a severe appearance. But she was very friendly and exceptionally beloved among her people. In Baden-Baden she lived in the Hôtel de Russie, and at other times in her palace at Karlsruhe or in Salem.

At that time many Russians came to Baden-Baden to take cures, and many of them even had their own houses which they occupied during the summer. I remember two aged Princesses Garagin, who had been friends of my grandfather when he was young and had an old and pretty house on the Oos. Every Sunday the Russian colony was brought together by a fine Russian orchestra ; Grandpapa too used to go regularly to hear it on days when he was well.

I enjoyed to the full the beautiful walks I had through the gardens, along the Lichtentaler Allee or up to the old castle. We had some marvellously lovely excursions to the enchanting little rococo Castle Favorite, lying in the Rhine plain amid flowery meadows and blossoming fruit trees, or up the Iburg or to the fine Castle Ebersteinburg. From here there was a magnificent view across the

188

mountains and valleys of the Black Forest ; on clear days
one could even see from the top as far as Strassburg,
lying in the misty distance. The young leaves of the
beeches were brilliant in the first green of May, and the
fruit trees were a sea of white and pink blossom. Rhodo-
dendrons and azaleas bloomed in the parks, and
wisterias fell in blue cascades from the houses and stone
walls, giving the town a southern character in its riot of
blossom. Listening to the good concerts in front of the
Kurhaus, and strolling through the arcades past the
beautiful shop-windows, also gave me great pleasure, so
that these visits to Baden form a particularly pleasant
recollection of my youth. But in my recollections of that
period the external surroundings are always less vivid
than the memory of my grandfather, which fills the
foreground ; even during those days his kindness of heart
towards me remained unchanged.

*

In the year 1904 I was at Michailovskoe for the last
time ; my betrothal took place shortly after our return to
Gelbensande. In August of that summer the ardently-
desired heir to the throne was born, little Grand Duke
Alexei. This event caused great and sincere joy throughout Russia, and countless hopes were centred on the life
of this poor little boy, who seemed destined one day to
be the ruler of Russia. The parents were extremely
delighted, especially as the Tsarina had four times
presented her spouse with daughters instead of the
expected heir to the throne. For the Tsarina the event

meant also an increased prestige among the people, and
therefore seemed to be the beginning of a happier time.
Prince Heinrich of Prussia came to Peterhof for the
christening on August 24 as the representative of the
Kaiser, who was one of the godparents together with
King Edward, my grandfather and other royalties. As
I already had some inkling of my impending betrothal
it was naturally of considerable interest to me to meet the
uncle of my future husband. He was popular with
everyone, including the Russian Court, and was received
everywhere with great affection.

Shortly after this the German courier arrived at
Michailovskoe with the letter from my future father-
in-law to my mother which was of such significance for
my future life, and I spent this last visit to my grandfather with the realisation that it was a farewell visit,
and with feelings very different from those of the past.

Through this summer too we experienced great concern over the Russo-Japanese war, and the hopes and
fears which were felt particularly for the beleaguered
town of Port Arthur. Dark clouds were then descending
on the Russian Empire.

I remember that one day we went with Their Majesties
to a parade-ground not far from Peterhof where troops
for the front were to receive a blessing. We drove in carriages round the battalions, and as we passed the
Tsarina distributed sacred medals and ikons. I shall
never forget the sight of those mud-grey figures, in full
field-kit, who had to stand in pools of water owing to the
heavy rain which had fallen. The slow playing of the

imperial anthem gave it all an intensely melancholy effect, which was deepened when one thought how many thousand versts the poor men had to go before they would reach the theatre of war in Eastern Asia—and what a fate was awaiting them ! Most of them hardly knew what it was all about, and why they had been torn away from their families and their fields. How different, on the contrary, was the full consciousness of the justice of their cause and the enthusiasm with which our German troops went out in 1914 !

We also paid a visit to the Baltic fleet in Kronstadt, before it set out on its voyage nearly round the globe to meet its end at Tshushima, and we went once again on board our beloved *Svietlana* to say farewell. How different she looked then from the former occasions when she had come to take us on those happy voyages ! The woodwork had all been removed owing to the danger of fire, and both on the decks and in the cabins there was only bare iron and steel. We spent a last few happy hours with the esteemed commander, Captain von Scheine, and his wife, *née* Princess Urusoff. Captain von Scheine presented me on that occasion with the picture of Christ already mentioned, which always orna-mented my cabin and had now also been removed on account of its wooden frame. I accepted it with deep gratitude, and have always given it a place of honour in my bedroom.

When the fleet was on its way to the theatre of war in the East, Frau von Scheine came to stay with us at Cannes, thinking that she might perhaps be able to see her husband once more. But her hope that she might be able to visit him during the long stay of the fleet at Madagascar was not destined to be fulfilled. She never saw her dear husband again : on the morning of May 28th, 1905, he went down with his gallant little cruiser in the naval battle of Tshushima. Some time afterwards my husband gave me a picture by the artist Bohrdt depicting the sinking of our brave *Svietlana* in her fight against two Japanese cruisers. I remember that this picture affected me deeply, and that I burst into tears when I saw it so unexpectedly. Frau von Scheine, who after many hardships following on the Russian revolution now lives abroad with her mother, has remained a faithful friend of mine. In this way my dear friends still link me with the past which has gone for ever.

On this last visit to Kronstadt we also saw an ironclad which had just been completed, the *Tsar Alexander III.* She was a vessel of about 14,000 tons with four 30.5 cm. guns, and she was peculiarly high in her build, with high sides. It made me feel that if she sank the crew would be helplessly trapped, as though in a great coffin. Our German ships with their wide clear decks were on the contrary extremely open. The Russian ships, except for a few new cruisers, were of old types, and it is in itself a marvel how Admiral Rozjestvenski ever succeeded in getting all those diverse units right out to the Far East. The Admiral came to Michailovskoe to pay my mother a farewell visit shortly before his departure. I can still see the kindly and intelligent man in his black naval uniform. He was severely wounded and was a prisoner-of-war in Japan after the battle of Tshushima.

After that visit I was only once again in Russia, in 1911, for the official visit already mentioned to the Tsar and Tsarina at Tsarskoe Selo.

CHAPTER X

MY BETROTHAL

In the autumn of the year 1903 my brother and I
visited our sister Alexandrine at Fredensborg in Zeeland,
and this was the prelude to an important event in our
family. The famous royal palace of Denmark is situated
at Fredensborg, on the shores of the wooded lake of
Esrom, in the midst of a wonderful park intersected by
long avenues of trees.

To our surprise and delight we were met at Fredensborg station by the aged King Christian IX himself, and
he was so kind to us that he won our hearts on the spot.
And afterwards when we were taken into the great salon
of the palace, where members of the royal family and
their entourage were assembled to receive us (sometimes
a very painful moment for young people), the Tsarina
Marie Feodorovna, whom we already knew well, was the
first to come forward to welcome us with the greatest
kindness and cordiality. All sense of constraint was immediately banished, and there was no occasion for any
awkwardness or embarrassment. We very soon felt completely at home among the many members of the Danish
royal family.

Probably there has seldom been such a patriarchal
relationship and such close intimacy in any royal family
as in the Danish family at the time of King Christian IX.

The old King was always the spiritual centre of his circle, beloved by children and grandchildren. He was slim and active, though not very tall, and had preserved his youthfulness up to extreme old age ; in spite of his eighty-four years he used to take two or three rides every morning. He was known as " the father-in-law of Europe," and was in fact father-in-law of King Edward VII of Great Britain through his daughter Alexandra, and through his daughter Dagmar, whose Russian name was Maria Feodorovna, father-in-law of the Tsar Alexander III. His third daughter, Princess Thyra, was the wife of the Duke of Cumberland. Every autumn the kinsfolk from England and from Russia used to meet at Fredensborg, where they shared a happy family life. It is said that in the course of these family gatherings many conversations took place which had their influence on high politics. I cannot express any opinion about that, as I was much too young at the time.

To my intense delight the family of the Duke of Cumberland, with whom we had made great friends in Cannes, were also staying at Fredensborg and we soon formed a very happy party ; we spent the time chiefly in bicycling, which was just coming into fashion, and in merry games in the great park. This happy and informal intercourse led to the engagement of my brother and the second daughter of the Duke of Cumberland, a little before Christmas.

My brother could not have formed any alliance which would have been more welcome to my mother and to us sisters. For years the Cumberland family had been among our closest friends, and his future bride had long ago found a place in all our hearts. Henceforth Alix became our beloved sister and in this has never changed through all the years of joy or sorrow up to the present day. And she has kept up our ancestral home with such affectionate understanding that we could not imagine anything more perfect ; for this we are particularly grateful to her.

As my mother allowed me to spend Christmas at Gmunden with the betrothed couple I had a special opportunity of appreciating my brother's happiness. Even the journey through the snow-covered Alps gave me new delight, all the greater because for me such sights were quite unaccustomed. The days that I was able to spend at Gmunden with the engaged couple, my friend Olga and the other members of that beloved family, were indescribably beautiful. I cannot express the enthusiasm I felt at the mere sight of the snow !

The King of Denmark was also present, with his brother, Hans von Holstein-Glücksburg, in order to celebrate Christmas with his daughter's family. On Christmas Eve the Queen of Hanover, mother of the Duke of Cumberland, also came over from her villa near-by, with her youngest daughter, Mary. Her son gave her some magnificent diamond ear-rings for a Christmas present, and she was so immensely pleased with them that she seized King Christian, her equal in age and youthfulness, by the arm, and waltzed round the room with him amid the applause of the whole assembled company.

At the beginning of January my brother and I left the hospitable Cumberland residence in order to spend Mama's name-day, the fourth of January, with her in Cannes. Soon afterwards my brother had the happiness of receiving his betrothed and her family there for a visit of some weeks, and we were able once more to enjoy joint excursions on sea and land. It was very opportune for us that the representative of the Daimler Works, Herr Jellinek, placed at the disposal of the engaged couple an immense red limousine. As my brother had already driven a Mercedes for several years our connections with this world-famous firm are of long standing. It was, by the way, Mercedes, the daughter of Herr Jellinek, who gave the firm this well-known name.

In the middle of May we received the sad news of the sudden death of my cousin Paul Friedrich who, together with his sister Marie Antoinette and his brother Heinrich Borwin, had been among our favourite playmates. He was a naval lieutenant, and was the victim of an accident at Kiel. With him something of the golden youth we had shared was buried in an early grave.

When we arrived at Gmunden at the beginning of June for my brother's wedding, we found the whole family there in the deepest grief. Aunt Mary had died quite suddenly from appendicitis. As some of the wedding guests had already arrived it was decided not to postpone the ceremony, in spite of this great sorrow. In view of this sad event there could not, of course, be any festive celebrations on the eve of the wedding, and the day of the ceremony itself passed in solemn mood

197

without gaiety. Services were held each evening at Queen Marie's villa, the house of mourning. An excursion across the beautiful Traunsee gave me the only cheerful impression that I carried away with me. Under these circumstances my mother and I left the Cumberland house on the day after the wedding, for Mecklenburg. For the home-coming of the young couple to Schwerin was to follow a few weeks later.

The Gordon–Bennett International Motor Races, which took place on the 17th of June, 1904, between Homburg-von-der-Höhe and Saalburg, were to play in my own fate the same part that our visit to Denmark in the previous year had played for my brother. My mother, who attended the races as patroness of the German Automobile Club, had taken me with her, to my great delight, and the anticipations I had cherished were not disappointed. As a society occasion it was supremely brilliant; Their Majesties were present with their suites, as well as a great number of royal personages. As the track was laid so that the whole of it was open to view, it was possible to follow the course of the races in every detail. It was desperately exciting when the cars dashed round the difficult bends, first one and then another taking the lead. We were glad when the German competitors gained ground, but we applauded wholeheartedly the French motorist who was the final victor.

Some time after the racing had begun, General von Plessen, the Kaiser's well-known adjutant-general, came to our box in order to invite my mother and me, in the name of Their Majesties, to visit the royal box. This was the second occasion on which I met my future parents-in-law. This time the Kaiserin had a very intimate and significant talk with me. Her kindness and motherliness gave her conversation such warmth of feeling that my heart was at once filled with affection and respect for her. But I was not altogether conscious of the importance those moments were to have in shaping my future life.

When the ceremonial entry of my brother and my sister-in-law into Schwerin took place at the beginning of July, the large number of royal guests who came to celebrate the occasion included the Crown Prince ; he acted as deputy for his imperial father, and presented the beautiful wedding gift from the Kaiser and Kaiserin, a service made at the royal porcelain factory in Berlin. Until then I had never met the Crown Prince, but I could very well picture to myself his outward appearance, his manner and the unaffected spontaneity which won universal praise.

I shall never forget how, on the afternoon of July 5th, the day of the ceremony, standing on the White Staircase with my mother and sister to receive the guests, I saw my future husband coming up the steps ; for me the first moment settled everything ! Brief as his stay was, it was full of new experience for us both. In the midst of all the social functions of the first day : dinner, concert and dramatic performance, we still managed to find opportunity for quiet conversation in which we could make each other's acquaintance.

The next day we were able to pursue it further. In

the morning we rode together, accompanied by my brother-in-law Christian and my aunt Charlotte Reuss as " gooseberries "—for it went without saying that such an ardent horseman as the Crown Prince wanted to ascertain how the woman he had chosen could " sit a horse." In the afternoon there was one more unforgettable expedition across the lake to Grandmama Marie's, where Queen Wilhelmine was staying, and in the evening after a state concert another happy meeting at supper, and then irrevocably the hour of parting struck. The Crown Prince took his leave, and the rest of the festivities had lost all interest for me ! Even my first Court ball, which took place at this time, and a wonderful garden-party in the castle grounds failed to make me forget that there was something missing.

Soon after that the Crown Prince and I met for the second time. When we stopped in Berlin on our last journey to Russia, he had supper with us at the " Kaiserhof " and then drove us in his car through the Tiergarten to the station. From that day on I saw everything, as the saying is, through rose-coloured spectacles.

Some weeks later my mother received by courier at Michailovskoe the memorable letter from the Kaiser mentioned above, in which he sought my hand in marriage for his son. The courier who brought the letter from the German Embassy in St. Petersburg was von Stünzner, who was then king's messenger ; a year later he entered the service of the Crown Prince as head-forester and became our much-esteemed chief-ranger at Öls. We still see him to-day as the messenger of love, the

ENTRY OF THE CROWN PRINCE INTO BERLIN, JUNE 3, 1905

THE BRIDAL COACH AT THE PARISER PLATZ

diplomatic bearer of that highly important letter of twenty-five years ago.

I had long ago made up my mind what my answer would be, if my mother were to ask me ; but I had also fully considered the duties I should be taking upon myself. I knew whose place I was some day to fill, and realised the difficulty of the task and the responsibility which it involved in the sight of God and of a great people. The succession of Prussian Queens from Queen Luise to our present Kaiserin rose before my eyes : should I be worthy of them ? I thought it all over, and then questioned my heart once again, and answered my mother gladly : " Yes."

From that day forward I was conscious of an intense but happy restlessness. I had to keep myself very severely in hand, because the impending engagement was to be kept strictly secret. In this we were extraordinarily successful, although as a rule the press and the public are aware of royal engagements long before the event. But how great was my happiness in anticipation when Mama told me, on our way back to Germany at the end of August, that the Crown Prince was to visit us at Gelbensande within the next few days ! Now indeed the great event was to become an actual fact !

*

Early in the morning of September 3, the Crown Prince arrived with my Danish brother and sister at the dear old hunting-box at Gelbensande. He was accompanied by his adjutant, Captain von Stülpnagel, who afterwards became my chamberlain, and has remained our trusted friend through good and evil days. The Crown Prince had my brother's bachelor room, above my balcony—in bygone years many a glass of water had been poured down there, on our sisterly heads !

When Mama and I had taken our guest to his room and were coming down the stairs again, we found sitting down below, looking very desolate and thoroughly melancholy, a small black dog, a black-and-tan terrier. In reply to my mother's astonished inquiry as to what this dog was—for he was not among the guests whose arrival had been announced—she was told by one of the servants that it was the Crown Prince's dog. This was my first meeting with the faithful Trick, who henceforth shared our daily life for ten years. He was quite a character, and was extremely devoted to his master ; it was only after at least two years that he recognised me as belonging to him, but after that he was as much attached to me as to my husband. Because of his extraordinary devotion we used to call him our familiar spirit.

In the morning of that memorable day, September 4th, the Crown Prince and I had a wonderful ride, never to be forgotten, and after lunch we drove to the tea-house and amused ourselves in our canoes on the sea. Numbers of visitors from Graal and Müritz assembled meanwhile on the shore, and waved enthusiastically to the Crown Prince and the rest of us. I must take this opportunity to state that we did not become engaged at the tea-house, as everybody said at the time.

After a beautiful drive back in the twilight stillness of

the evening, it was at home that we plighted our troth. Together we went to my mother, as an engaged couple, and asked for her blessing, which she gave us joyfully and with great emotion.

Of course it was impossible now to keep the secret any longer. My dear sister and brother-in-law were told first, and then my mother gave the news to all our faithful household, and the radiant faces of our retainers, most of whom had known me from my childhood, bore witness to their heartfelt interest in the joyful event.

Then came the question of informing Their Majesties and my brother, who were at Altona for the manœuvres. Our telegram arrived while the parade dinner was in progress, and was immediately announced by the Kaiser. The Kaiserin, as my brother told me, received the news with visible emotion—and indeed it meant the future fate of her beloved eldest son !

The next day numerous bearers of congratulations began to arrive at the forest retreat of Gelbensande ; the school-children from Ribnitz came in a long procession to wish us joy, and this pleased us particularly. My brother and sister-in-law came from Altona to rejoice with us in our happiness. And then by post and by wire streams of good wishes poured into the house ; I believe two thousand telegrams alone were received. The little post-office at Gelbensande had never known such days ! Mama arranged a convenient place in my father's writing-room for us, where we could read and reply to the messages of congratulation without interruption ; or rather, where we might have read them and replied to them. For I must regretfully admit that the number of messages we answered personally remained extremely modest.

Blissful, unforgettable days of new-found happiness !

*

The delightful days passed all too quickly, and then we all had to go to Schwerin for the imperial manœuvres. The Crown Prince, who was then Captain of the Second Company of the First Guards Regiment, took up his quarters at Zippendorf, a place quite close to Schwerin.

The Kaiser and Kaiserin were expected the next day. My mother drove with the Crown Prince and me to the junction at Kleinen ; there we joined the royal state train. My future parents-in-law received me most cordially ; the Kaiserin was just like a mother to me, and always remained so to the end of her life. At the station at Schwerin Their Majesties had a great reception. The Kaiser and my brother inspected the guard of honour, while the royal ladies exchanged greetings. Then came the drive to the castle : the Kaiser in the Daumont carriage with my brother, the Kaiserin with my sister-in-law, and Mama with us, the betrothed couple. The people of Schwerin greeted us with the most cordial and touching enthusiasm !

Next came the manœuvres, to which we generally drove out early each morning. On the last day, when the co-operation of the fleet, which disembarked a landing corps, provided a special attraction, the Kaiserin took my sister-in-law Alix and me to the parade-ground near Wismar ; there we found the Crown Prince with his regiment, and to our delight were able to speak to him in an interval of the manœuvres. My sister-in-law had been taking part in the manœuvres on horseback most of the time in her smart dragoon's uniform—she was Colonel of the Second Mecklenburg Grand-Ducal Dragoon Regiment No. 18 ; sitting next to my brother in the carriage, she had more than once been taken for the Grand Duke's aide-de-camp, to her great satisfaction.

On a certain evening that we spent in the family circle at the Schwerin castle, during the manœuvres, the date of our wedding was arranged. Their Majesties had at first wished that a long engagement should be avoided and that our marriage should take place in November. My mother, however, was afraid that the winter, which I should have to spend in Germany after my marriage, might be bad for me, as hitherto I had spent every winter in the south. So the time was fixed for the spring or early summer of the following year. The exact date which was decided on later had eventually to be postponed for a fortnight, because the Kaiserin, who was then at Wiesbaden, slipped on a winding staircase, and broke her arm. The date finally appointed for the wedding was June 6.

For us this naturally meant a painful period of waiting, as well as a long separation, as I was to go to Cannes once more for the winter. But the Crown Prince appreciated Mama's reasons, and so we submitted to this ruling, though with heavy hearts.

*

In the middle of October I paid my first visit to my future parents-in-law at Potsdam. My brother and sister-in-law accompanied me on the journey to my future home.

On a gloriously clear autumn evening we arrived at Wildpark. We drove in an open carriage through the great iron gate and along the beautiful road to the New Palace glowing in the evening light. The impression of those hours will remain with me always unforgotten : the magnificent castle, the affection of my parents-in-law, who received me as their daughter, my fiancé radiant with happiness, and his little sister Viktoria Luise, the sunshine of the house, who, bubbling over with delight, immediately christened me " Cilly " and became a dear companion of mine ; and then all those surrounding the Kaiser and Kaiserin, who welcomed me with open arms ; my magnificent rooms in the so-called royal apartments, which since then have always been the rooms used by royal brides-to-be ; and everywhere the most wonderful flowers from the hot-houses of Sanssouci. I felt as if I had been bewitched.

Life in the New Palace seemed to me extremely pleasant. In the morning we used to ride or to go for walks in the beautiful parks or for longer excursions into the idyllic country round Potsdam. One evening too we went to the Royal Theatre in Berlin, where I was, so to speak, introduced to the Berlin public ; to my joy, we were very warmly received. I was able to observe with keen satisfaction on this and other occasions the great popularity enjoyed by the Crown Prince in Berlin and Potsdam. How they applauded when he marched through the town with his Company or rode past on his fine thoroughbred ! In addition to my deep personal happiness I felt intense pride in the consciousness of being betrothed to the darling of the German people.

Guests from the sphere of art, science or politics often dined at the New Palace, and the Kaiser used to talk with them in his vivacious way, taking an interest in everything. The chief subject of political conversation at the time was the Russo-Japanese war, particularly the strange incident at the Dogger-bank, when the Russian fleet on its way to the Far East fired on an English fishing fleet, under the impression that they were Japanese torpedo-boats. Conversation at the New Palace was quite unconstrained, and everyone could express freely what he felt.

Perhaps the loveliest hour of the day came at tea-time, when we used to sit cosily and quietly with the Kaiserin, while a cheerful fire crackled on the hearth. Sometimes my brother-in-law Eitel-Friedrich or one of the younger brothers would join us at this hour, but generally we two were alone with the Kaiserin. Then we used to have long and absorbing conversations on all the questions that intimately concern a wife and mother, and I gained a growing insight into the soul of this woman, unique and unforgettable, in whom the family found its natural centre.

I used generally to sit near her on her comfortable sofa, where I felt very safe under her protection, and I kept this place of honour until the dark November days of 1918. Even to-day I never see the sofa, which is now at Doorn, without emotion and a grateful recollection of the happy hours I was permitted to spend, in the course of long years, with my dear mother-in-law.

It would touch on chords which are too sensitive if I were to put into words what the Kaiserin was to me in days of happiness and of gloom. For us, her own children and her children by marriage, she was, in one word : Mother. That expresses everything.

She was closest to me at the times when my children came into the world and she helped me with all her maternal care and forethought. If she came into the room, dressed all in white as she was at such times, and just laid her soft hand on my forehead, with her kindly and loving smile, I felt comforted in spite of all my uneasiness. And I think that for her it was a supremely happy moment when she could lay the new-born grandchild in my arms. How devoted she was afterwards in her care of me and my child—somewhat severe perhaps, according to modern notions, but success was on her side !

And in general how considerate the Kaiserin was for her daughters-in-law ! She was always afraid that we should tire ourselves, and would herself undertake a visit to some invalid or would attend some official function, so that we might not be over-fatigued.

In her personal relations with us the Kaiserin was kindness and courtesy itself. Except at formal Court functions whenever she went through a door she would always, by an affectionate gesture, make us go with her. She never sat down at meals or in any social gathering without making a sign to us to be seated at the same moment. Though she was indeed both mother and Empress her sympathetic tact prompted her to act in this way and not otherwise.

But in spite of her gentleness the Kaiserin could be very firm at times, if it was a question of carrying through what she considered right, in opposition to us children. She too stood at the cross-roads of the generations. She always upheld the observance of traditional forms, and never, except on trifling points, allowed her daughters-in-law to diverge from them. This often seemed hard to us at the time, but dark and difficult years have taught me to understand it.

I have already mentioned in passing that the Kaiserin gave special attention, based on her practical knowledge, to the question of infant welfare ; it was probably in this sphere that her nature found its fullest expression. But she had the well-being of young girls equally at heart. She obtained up-to-date information from leading specialists on all important and fundamental questions, especially on the growing demand for the higher education of girls, and often gave some direction or some piece of advice which sprang from the depths of her own maternal understanding.

The Kaiserin was untiring in her activities in the sphere of hospital work. The German national Frauen-Verein achieved great results under her guidance, and at the present day we can see in all directions how her benevolent sympathy and interest survive in works of Christian charity. She never spared herself when it was a question of visiting the sick or of alleviating suffering through some personal effort. Indeed, the severe heart-trouble from which she suffered was partly due to the fact that she never considered her own health when it was a question of fulfilling her national duties. And it was all done quietly and without much talk. The Kaiserin was by nature infinitely modest and she did good not for the sake of appearances, but because her gentle heart prompted her to it.

I cannot express how thankful I am, that in all her activities she was for me a peerless example, and that she influenced me by word and deed to follow her in the many branches of social work and beneficent effort in which she was indefatigable. It was in dealing with the practical affairs of charitable undertakings that we were so closely associated outside the family circle. I never see her form more vividly before my eyes than when I try, under the totally different conditions of to-day, to emulate her in the sphere of charity and to follow in her steps.

In this work I am gratefully conscious of her blessing.

The whole existence of the Kaiserin was filled with a deep and genuine piety. She clung with her whole soul to the Evangelical faith from which she received so much strength and courage. Without being bigoted or narrow-minded, she would let nothing weaken or explain away the word of God. The Christianity of which she and her august spouse were living examples to us all, was conceived and practised in a thoroughly German spirit, and their firm faith helped them in the difficult hours of their lives. It always stirs my emotions afresh when sometimes in some remote little village church, I am shown a Bible presented by my mother-in-law, in which she had written a beautiful text. These Bibles always seem to me to be living evidence of the strength of her faith and of her participation in the lives of her beloved people. Her Christian piety still lives for all to see in the Evangelical institution for women founded by her.

It would take me too far afield if I attempted to describe here all that the Kaiserin was to the German people through those long years. To all who knew her she appeared as the model of the German woman, and it is thus that her living image is always before my eyes.

*

After a fortnight of happy enjoyment at the New Palace I took my leave, full of profound gratitude for all the affection with which the Kaiser and Kaiserin had received me, and for all the kindness which had been shown to me by their circle, and especially by the ladies in attendance on the Kaiserin, Countess Brockdorff,

Countess Keller and Fräulein von Gersdorff. After stopping for a short time at Ludwigslust, I travelled to Baden-Baden, and there once more spent a happy time with my Russian grandfather and my Baden relatives.

But the greatest pleasure of all was given me by the Crown Prince. I knew that he was far away, hunting in Bavaria—and one morning he stood before me ! That was a wonderful moment ! Kind Miss King, who had been in the plot, had been as silent as the grave, so that the surprise was completely successful. My grandfather was delighted to have us both near him, and went for many drives with us in the glorious autumn weather, some short and some to more distant places. For my fiancé indeed it was sometimes a severe test of endurance to sit for several hours in the slow landau—I am thinking particularly of a drive to Schloss Favorite—and to feel that he was under the old gentleman's care. But we gladly made these little sacrifices—if they were sacrifices—in return for the great kindness and affection that he bestowed on us both !

But now began the dreaded period of separation. The Crown Prince went back to Potsdam, while I travelled with Grandpapa to Cannes for the winter. Daily letters kept us in close communication, but also made us miss one another all the more. The Crown Prince gave me great pleasure by having a life-sized portrait of himself painted for me by Vilma Parlaghy, so that at least I could have his image always with me.

At last, however, an opportunity of meeting again was to be arranged for us. But this was not so simple as it may seem. According to the views then prevailing it was extremely unusual for a Prussian Prince to meet his betrothed in a foreign country. When at last agreement had been reached in principle, Florence was selected as the meeting-place. But a new difficulty arose when, on the day before our intended journey, Mama was suddenly taken ill. It was proposed that a royal chaperon should come from Berlin, but at Mama's suggestion General von Maltzahn and his wife were approved, and had to travel post-haste from Schwerin.

I spent ten indescribably beautiful days with my fiancé in Florence. I stayed with my escort at the Grand Hotel on the Piazza Manin, the Crown Prince with his adjutants, Marshal von Trotha and Captain von Stülpnagel, in the hotel opposite.

In the square in front of my hotel, then as now, flower-sellers used to stand every morning, offering for sale in baskets the most lovely carnations, wallflowers, roses and other flowers. Each morning the Crown Prince used to buy a whole basket full of flowers, and come laden with it into my room. The happiness that a girl who is betrothed feels at such a moment may be recalled, perhaps, but certainly cannot be described ! On one occasion my fiancé surprised me by appearing not with a basket of flowers, but with a charming Italian Spitz ; he was snow-white, with a black nose and eyes, and his hair had been curled like a little lion. For years he was my faithful companion, and a living reminder of those lovely days in Florence.

Of course we visited galleries and the chief sights of

the wonderful city on the Arno. But I am afraid our attention, much to Miss King's distress, was not always fixed on the works of art we had come to see. To take an engaged couple to a museum is admittedly a thankless enterprise !

Twenty-two years later we once more visited Florence, which had always remained such a precious memory, and refreshed our early impressions. This time we stayed together at the Grand Hotel, and the proprietor gave us the same rooms that I had occupied in the old days. And although all the other rooms have been altered, the green corner-salon, in which we spent so many happy hours then, has remained unchanged. And so it seemed to us, at least for a few moments, that we were back again in the year 1904.

*

Soon after this began the period of leave-taking. First in Cannes. Mama gave a great soirée for all our acquaintances on the Riviera. I received endless good wishes for my approaching marriage, and numbers of beautiful presents were given to me. Numerous relations and friends were at the little station when we left, and gave me an ovation as enthusiastic as it was flattering.

I was to spend the last weeks before my marriage with my brother and sister in Schwerin. But as there was an outbreak of chicken-pox at the castle, Grandmama Marie invited me to Raben-Steinfeld. The Crown Prince frequently visited us there, and spent Easter with us. These weeks of our engagement, spent in the loving care of my grandmother, have remained among my most beautiful memories. In daily intercourse with her in her own house, I was able during those four weeks to become specially intimate with her.

I have already said that Grandmama Marie was a quiet, reserved and unassuming woman. Her greatness lay not in outward show and ostentation, but in her deeply sympathetic nature as wife and mother, and in her keen interest in social and charitable work, in which she resembled my mother-in-law. With her unpretentious and genuine disposition, her kind-heartedness and dignity, she was one of the women who have enhanced the honour of German royalty, one of those whose memory will live in the hearts of their family, and, in spite of all changes, in the hearts of their people.

What a vivid picture of the great days of my grandfather I was able to call up, not only from Grandmama's accounts, but also from her own actual life and conduct. Great days, because that was the period in which at last the ruling Houses of Germany buried their differences and created in the Empire a new form of state. But great days also because there were then living and working men who through the greatness of their human achievement won fame far beyond the bounds of their own country and, whether as Prince or scholar, general or teacher, showed the world the true greatness of Germany in creative intellect.

In those days too it was possible for royal personages like my grandfather and his life's companion to move

among their people without constraint, in the firm conviction of lasting mutual loyalty. How my grandmother
loved to tell of the walks she used to take through the
town with her husband and children, when they would
be greeted by everyone, and would often stop to chat
with one person and another, and to inquire sympathe-
tically how some individual and his family were getting
on ! The people of Mecklenburg might well have the
feeling that the royal pair took a parental interest in
their welfare, and that they could tell them frankly all
their troubles and anxieties.

Grandmama also told us a great deal about the war
period of 1870-71. Immediately after the outbreak of
war she had opened a great work-room at the castle,
where the ladies of Schwerin made and packed surgical
bandages to be sent to the front. The Marien-Frauen-
Verein (nursing association) dates from this time. She
particularly liked to tell us how she used to read aloud
my grandfather's letters from the front to her children
and her ladies, and with what tremendous enthusiasm
the news of victories was received in Mecklenburg.

During our own visit to Steinfeld she also constantly
received letters, which she read aloud to us in the evenings, to our great interest. There were letters from my
uncle Adolf Friedrich, who just at that time was making
an expedition through Africa. He too, like his father,
though in a different way, did honour to his country
and his rank by personal courage and outstanding
achievements.

Thus this month at Steinfeld was a time of great

THE CROWN PRINCE'S FAMILY IN 1927

[Photograph by W. Niederastroh, Potsdam

spiritual profit for me, and I look back on it with pleasure and gratitude.

Immediately afterwards I went with my brother and sister to Ludwigslust, our second residence not far from Schwerin. Our family frequently spent a few weeks in the spring and autumn at this magnificent palace, planned in the style of Louis XV. My future Mistress of the Robes, Baroness von Tiele-Winckler, *née* Countess von der Schulenburg, came there on this occasion, so that I had an opportunity of getting to know her before my marriage. I was greatly charmed from the first by her distinguished and winning personality and soon established a firm friendship with her, which has outlasted all the vicissitudes of time.

And now came the great parting from Schwerin, from the town and from the castle. As in accordance with Prussian Court precedent the wedding was to take place in Berlin, my brother arranged a number of social functions at Schwerin, so that the people of Mecklenburg might have an opportunity of taking leave of their young Duchess. A great ceremonial dinner to the militia, who came in their picturesque red uniforms, opened the proceedings, and a charming garden fête in the castle grounds, and other festivities, followed.

More and more farewells. My heart grew heavy. I had to say farewell to my beloved home, to people I loved who had cared for and cherished me in my childhood, and finally, to the castle which had been my childhood's home. Once more, quite alone, I went through all the rooms, climbed once more to Niklot's tower, listened once more to the striking of the clock, and finally, in silent contemplation at the last service in the castle chapel, sought strength and courage so that I might be equal to the new duties that awaited me. My deep happiness and confidence in a blissful future with the man I loved enabled me to get over the pain of the final parting.

On the morning of June 3, in brilliantly hot weather, I left Schwerin with Mama and my brother and sister. The friendly farewell greetings of the loyal people of Mecklenburg had accompanied me all the way to the station.

And now I was on the way to my new home.

CHAPTER XI

MY MARRIAGE

When I had crossed the Prussian frontier on my journey from Schwerin to Berlin I left the Mecklenburg special train at Wittenberge, where I first touched Prussian soil. Here I was received in the name of the Kaiser by the Marshal of the Court, Baron von Reischach, the Governor of the Palace Count von Hohenthal-Dölkau and the Chamberlain Count Kalnein-Kilgis. These gentlemen had been appointed as my official escort for the period of the marriage celebrations. General von Bülow, commanding the Third Army Corps, who was afterwards Commander-in-Chief in the world war, and the President of the Province of Brandenburg also took part in the reception, as well as the ladies of my new court : the Mistress of the Robes, Baroness von Tiele-Winckler, whom I already knew, the Chamberlain Count von Bismarck-Bohlen, and the two charming ladies-in-waiting, Countess Walpurgis of Dohna-Schlobitten, afterwards Frau von Mutius, and Fräulein Else Pauline of Helldorff, later Frau von Plessen. After the presentations, accompanied by the gentlemen of my escort I inspected the guard of honour of the 24th Infantry which was lined up at the station. For me it was a supremely solemn moment when I thus came in contact with the Prussian army in an official capacity for the first time.

In addition to the officials of my new household, the officers of the guard of honour and the heads of the local government, representatives of the Brandenburg nobility had also assembled on the platform, so that they might be the first to welcome their future Crown Princess on Brandenburg soil. Among them I met for the first time Baroness Lita von Putlitz who in later years became a very close friend of mine ; her friendship and loyalty to me have been maintained until the present day, so that I look back on that moment with profound gratitude.

I made the rest of the journey to Berlin in the imperial state train, while my brother and sister went on in their special train. According to Prussian court precedent it was only by a special concession that my mother was permitted to accompany me on the journey to Berlin beyond the frontier. On the way I had an opportunity of becoming better acquainted with the members of my new suite who had been chosen for me by Their Majesties and the Crown Prince. I liked them all extremely—and my first impression has been borne out by the fact that we have kept up the most cordial relations with one another long after the period of their official service came to an end.

A great reception took place on our arrival at the Lehrter station. " Roses, roses all the way " : this was the key-note of the decorations everywhere in the imperial capital. The station itself was hung with garlands of red roses inside and outside, I stepped through an archway decorated with garlands of roses to the state coach which was awaiting me, and roses were scattered along my route. How deeply touched I felt when, on the occasion of my recent silver wedding, I was sent a rose which had been carefully preserved ; how sorrowful the sight of it made me feel when I thought of the splendour and happiness of those days—and of all that has happened to us since then !

From the Lehrter station to Schloss Bellevue my mother drove in front with her escort, while I followed last of all in the state carriage with my ladies. All along the route there were roses, and on both sides countless throngs of people who welcomed me in a way that made my heart beat faster.

At Schloss Bellevue Their Majesties received me in full state, together with my own and the Crown Prince's relatives. When the carriage drove into the courtyard of the palace, the first company of the first Guards Regiment, who formed a guard of honour there, under the command of Prince Eitel Friedrich, presented arms, and the band played the parade march. The Kaiser helped me in his chivalrous way to alight from the carriage and welcomed me so warmly that my spirits rose, and then with him I inspected the Guards company. The soldiers with their tall figures and high brass helmets looked magnificent—it seemed as if the " long lads " of the days of Friedrich Wilhelm I had come to life again. Then my fiancé greeted me, the Kaiserin took me affectionately in her arms, and my mother and my brother and sister embraced me with deep emotion— I was happy to be surrounded by my family ! The Kaiserin's intense emotion was evident : to-day was to mark an important change in the fate of her beloved eldest son, and I was to be the first daughter-in-law who entered her house. What heartfelt prayers to God for our future and the future of the German people she must have uttered that day !

After an informal family lunch the Kaiser and the Princes left us ; the Crown Prince went to the Potsdamer station, in order to lead his Company from there to the royal palace, where he was to receive his bride. The people of Berlin greeted their Crown Prince with indescribable enthusiasm. At times he and his soldiers were almost unable to advance, notwithstanding the police cordons—the people of Berlin simply would not be held back, they would not suffer anyone to come between them and their Crown Prince. He was covered with showers of roses, his beautiful thoroughbred mare " Violet " was decorated with wreaths again and again and in the midst of increasing applause he and his Company almost had to force their way to the palace.

It was five o'clock in the afternoon when I left Schloss Bellevue, accompanied by the Kaiserin in that historic royal bridal coach, drawn by eight black horses. Actually it should have been the office of the eldest Princess of the House to accompany the bride on her ceremonial entry ; but the Kaiserin in her kind-heartedness insisted on being beside her first daughter-in-law on this memorable journey. Frau von Tiele-Winckler, Mistress of the Robes, sat opposite to us in the carriage. In accordance with Court etiquette she too, like the Kaiserin and myself, was in full evening dress.

Our procession was headed by forty postillons playing "Wir winden dir den Jungfern Kranz" and other cheerful melodies. They were followed, according to old custom, by the mounted corps of the Berlin butchers' guild, then a squadron of the first Dragoon Guards, with trumpeters at their head. Count Bassewitz, the Mecklenburg Minister of State, and the gentlemen of my escort, followed in three carriages each drawn by six horses. Immediately in front of my carriage rode a half-squadron of Life Guards, on my right Count Wedel, the chief equerry, and on the left side of the carriage the commander of the accompanying squadron of Life Guards. On the steps of the carriage stood royal pages ; in front rode two equerries. At the end of the procession came the other half squadron of Life Guards, the carriages of the Kaiserin's ladies and my ladies, and finally a squadron of the Second Lance-Guards, also with trumpeters at their head. It was the most magnificent display that the Berlin Court could provide.

The scenes which revealed themselves before my eyes from the Schloss Bellevue along the Berliner Chaussee to the Brandenburg Gate and Unter den Linden are indelibly impressed on my memory. Red roses again adorned my path. Tall poles had been set up everywhere and wreathed with roses ; from tree to tree and from one pole to another hung garlands of red roses. And on both sides were the people of Berlin who greeted me with irrepressible applause and enthusiasm ; the excessive heat of the June day had in no way deterred them from many hours of waiting. Particularly unforgettable were the troops of school children, who were drawn up between Bellevue and the Kleiner Stern. The charming sight of their fresh young faces and their childlike pleasure touched me indescribably.

Deeply stirred, I greeted the people on all sides continually, and felt sincere gratitude for the overwhelmingly enthusiastic reception accorded to me, to my joyful surprise, by the inhabitants of the capital. When I recalled those hours, how vividly I was always reminded of the words of Queen Luise, who, some years after her entry into Berlin, wrote to her brother Georg :

" Do you remember the solemnity of this day, how my heart beat with apprehension as I drew nearer to the gates of Berlin and received all the demonstrations of joy and honour, which I then deserved only through my firm resolve to do all that lay in my power to make my future husband happy and, if it might be, fortunate, and thereby to deserve the applause of these good people ? Ah yes, dear friend, that was a solemn hour for me, in which I became a citizen of Berlin ! "

Exactly the same unexpressed feeling had filled my heart too, when I approached the Brandenburg Gate and saw all those gay scenes passing by as if in a dream. At the Pariser Platz, as I knew, official Berlin was awaiting me.

Very soon this moment arrived. The guns fired a salute as we drove through the Brandenburg Gate, the procession halted and the window of the carriage was lowered. Here the Lord Mayor was waiting with the magistrates and many other officials, and greeted me in the name of the municipality and residents of Berlin. He recalled the arrival of Queen Luise, who was also a Mecklenburg Princess, and expressed the wish that my entry might bring happiness to me and to the royal family, to the city of Berlin and to our whole country. The words of thanks in which I replied saying that the remembrance of this wonderful reception would always remain alive in my heart, have proved absolutely true.

The procession moved on again, passing now down the time-honoured " Via triumphalis " of Prussia, Unter den Linden, between the double lines of troops, past the houses gay with flags and flowers, to the Palace of the Old Kaiser, to the opera-house, and then past the Palace of the Crown Prince, that historic building which Frederick the Great had occupied in his young days, where Queen Luise had lived and where the Kaiser and Kaiserin Friedrich had led the social and artistic life of Berlin during the long period when he was Crown Prince. This Palace was now to be my home, our home, and we grew so fond of it in the course of the long happy years that I shall probably never quite get over its loss.

The church-bells began to ring, salutes were fired : we were approaching the Palace. In the courtyard the Crown Prince gave the order for his company, which was drawn up there, to present arms. In the vestibule we were received by the Kaiser and the Princes of the House, and were conducted to the Hall of Knights where all the royal relatives were already assembled. How glad I was when I saw among them my dear old great-aunt of Baden, and she greeted me. Then followed the greetings of the many royal guests. Among my relations, besides the whole Mecklenburg family, my uncle Nikolai, the Grand Duke Michail Alexandrovich and my aunt Miechen, the Grand Duchess Vladimir, had come from Russia. After the presentations Their Majesties went with me on to the balcony of the hall overlooking the courtyard, and we looked on while the Crown Prince's company marched past with the Prince at their head. It was a scene that made my heart beat fast with happiness.

After the signing of the marriage contracts had been completed in the Kurfürsten hall, my mother and I were taken to our rooms. We occupied the apartments known as the suite of King Friedrich Wilhelm IV and I had the adjoining beautiful rococo bedroom of Frederick the Great as my bedroom. It was a unique sensation for me to occupy the great king's room, and I thought I could take it as a happy omen.

In the evening, when after the family dinner we went and stood at the window, we were again greeted with cheers and the waving of hats and handkerchiefs by the people of Berlin, who had assembled in thousands in the courtyard of the Palace. When I went to bed that night it was with the happy knowledge that I had been gladly received by the people to whom I was henceforth to belong.

The next day, a Sunday, there was a service in the Cathedral, in which Their Majesties and all the guests took part. I was deeply stirred when the first Chaplain of the Court, Dr. Dryander, preached on the text of the Apostle Paul : " Bear ye one another's burdens," and at the end the congregation sang " So nimm denn meine Hände."

On the evening of this day there was a great ceremonial dinner in the White Hall. For us ladies this was a very strenuous occasion, because our movements were very much hampered by our heavy velvet trains. We could not walk at all unless the trains were carried by two pages, and during dinner the trains had to be spread out over the backs of the chairs.

It was a scene of magical beauty that was presented on such evenings in the brilliantly-lighted halls of the royal palaces. Under Kaiser Wilhelm II the Berlin Court was certainly one of the best conducted in Europe. Count August Eulenburg, Lord Marshal of the Court and Marshal of the Household, its clever and discreet guide, was recognised by all Courts as an authority on questions of etiquette. A *grand seigneur* from head to foot, he used to move through the rooms with his staff of office on ceremonial occasions, directing everything politely but firmly and carrying out the commands of his imperial master with infinite dignity.

Perhaps in an age like the present, which has adopted the code of the new realism, people may smile at court convention and court pageantry. But even to-day we still see, for example at the wedding of the Italian Crown Prince recently celebrated with the greatest magnificence, that a people who believe in monarchy understand and approve the observance by their hereditary royal family of traditional customs and precedents on great occasions, involving the use of picturesque formalities and even a certain amount of display. It was in this spirit that important court functions in Berlin were always carried out. They were full of distinction and dignity, even magnificent, but never extravagant. By means of the most scrupulous economy in ordinary life a certain expenditure was possible on special occasions.

After the ceremonial dinner we listened to the music and tattoos from the Lustgarten. When we went to the windows we saw a torchlight procession of students from Berlin and Charlottenburg approaching, to the strains of the York march. It presented a wonderful scene, as they moved across the Lustgarten in curving lines, the torch-bearers on foot and the officers in full dress on horseback or in carriages, carrying the banners of the students' clubs ; the officers stood up in their carriages to salute us, flourishing their sabres and dipping their banners, while ceaseless cheering thundered from their young throats. Of all the ovations we received during those days, this remains in my memory as one of the most beautiful.

*

In the morning of Monday the fifth of June we held a reception, at which the Kaiserin was present, in the Braunschweig Gallery. For two hours we were receiving successive deputations of Corporations and Clubs bringing us addresses of greeting and wedding presents. The painted dessert service which was presented to us by a

group of 450 of the smaller municipalities was particularly enchanting. It was all an overwhelming testimony
to the loyalty of all classes to the royal family, and to the
friendliness which was shown towards us on all sides.
The intense heat, which lasted for some time longer,
made the continuous standing at this and other formal
functions extremely exhausting.

That evening, the " Polterabend," there was a gala
performance at the Royal Opera House in Unter den
Linden ; the programme was the first act from *Lohengrin*, conducted by Dr. Karl Muck, and the third act
from the *Meistersinger*, conducted by Dr. Richard
Strauss. The auditorium of the opera-house was a wonderful sight : garlands of roses and carnations, in the
finest gradations from the deepest red to pale yellow,
festooned the galleries and decorated the fronts of the
boxes. The beautiful dresses of the women, with their
magnificent jewellery, together with the brilliant uniforms, completed the picturesque and festal scene. In
the interval there was an informal reception in which I
made the acquaintance of a number of ladies and gentlemen of society and of the Ministries. The friendliness
which they all showed me was so encouraging that I
found the presentations much less trying than I had
feared.

The following morning, my wedding-morning, is
indelibly impressed on my memory. The sixth of June
was again a beautifully bright and hot summer day. At
an early hour my betrothed came to morning coffee,
with a gigantic bouquet of red roses in his arms. A little

later the Imperial Chancellor, Bülow, who had just become a prince, came to present himself to us in his new rank. Then the Japanese prince, Arisugava, and his wife were announced ; they came to make the formal presentation of the gifts from the Emperor of Japan. This occasioned a peculiar situation, inasmuch as my mother, who was in fact a Russian Grand Duchess, and the Japanese took no notice of each other—for Russia and Japan were still at war with one another ! The Crown Prince was able to stay while we received these guests, but afterwards he had to leave us, in conformity with an old Prussian custom in accordance with which the bridegroom had to remain away from the bride on their wedding day. I stayed within the inmost ring of my family, having lunch with Mama and Uncle Nikolai, and then trying to rest until the grand robing began.

A very complicated procedure was involved before my gorgeous dress of silver brocade was put on me ; the train, embroidered with silver myrtle, was not less than four metres long and indescribably heavy. When I was ready the time had come for me to say farewell to those of our faithful Mecklenburg servants who had accompanied us to Berlin. Then my heart began to grow heavy, but I made a brave effort to keep back my tears, for I really could not let my bridegroom see traces of tears on his bride's face.

Towards four o'clock the Crown Prince came to our room, and the four young ladies arrived who were to carry my train. These were, in addition to my two ladies-in-waiting, Fräulein Elizabeth von Trotha, daughter of our Marshal, and Countess Irma von Kanitz ; my Mistress of the Robes had to walk on the right of my train, and my Chamberlain, Count von Bismarck-Bohlen, on the left. The Crown Prince gave me his arm, and the procession began to move. We went first to a small room, the so-called Chinese Cabinet, where for generations the royal princess's crown had been placed on the heads of Prussian brides ; it was escorted by an officer and two men of the Life Guards, who never let it out of their sight during the time that I was wearing it. Here in the Chinese Cabinet the Kaiserin, assisted by her Mistress of the Robes, Countess von Brockdorff, with her own hands placed the crown on my head and put on me the historic jewels. The beautiful gold dressing-set of Queen Luise was used in making the crown secure.

From the Chinese Cabinet we passed on to the Kur-fürsten Room. There, in the presence of my parents-in-law, my mother and my brother and sister, the civil marriage was carried out by the Minister of the Royal Household, von Wedel, who on such occasions functioned as registrar. Here for the first time I signed my new name : Crown Princess of the German Empire and of Prussia. I have always particularly liked this double name, which has always been a reminder to me of my obligation to serve with all my strength not only my more limited country of Prussia but also the wider German Fatherland.

In the meanwhile all the guests had assembled in the halls and galleries. After the civil ceremony had been completed, they all joined the wedding procession, which took its course through the famous and historical rooms towards the chapel. Many friends who did not belong to the Court circle had taken up a position in the picture-gallery. The Castle Guards, composed of veterans of the war of 1870-71, were lined up in the White Hall, in their old uniform of the time of King Frederick II, and they presented arms with their rifles to the side. There too were all the officers of the First Guards Regiment, to which the Crown Prince belonged.

When we entered the palace chapel we were welcomed by the magnificent singing of the cathedral choir. The first Chaplain of the Court, Dr. Dryander, gave the wedding-address, for which he took as his text the words of the Book of Ruth : " Whither thou goest, I will go ; and where thou lodgest, I will lodge : thy people shall be my people, and thy God my God." The preacher interpreted the text in impressive words in its application to us, and then he performed the marriage-ceremony. As we exchanged rings, the salute of thirty-six guns began to thunder out from the Lustgarten ; it was fired by the first battery of the First Guards Field Artillery Regiment. After a prayer, Our Father and a blessing the solemn ceremony was over : I belonged to my beloved husband, I belonged to the Prussian Royal House.

After receiving the congratulations of the Kaiser and Kaiserin and Princes in the picture-gallery, we went to the White Hall, where the levee was to be held. We took our places between the Kaiser and Kaiserin under the canopy of the throne, with the royal guests on the right and left of the throne. Then the guests who had been invited began to file past us in a long unbroken line, the bands meanwhile playing polonaises, marches and songs. It was a wonderful sight to see, the ladies with their trains now spread out and with their brilliant jewels, and the gentlemen in their gay uniforms, all bowing low as they passed us.

After the conclusion of the levee the procession, which had to re-form, moved through the picture-gallery and the banqueting halls beyond, till it reached the Hall of Knights where the wedding banquet was to take place. In accordance with ancient usage the highest officials of the Court—Prince von Radolin as Lord High Steward, the Duke of Trachenberg, Cup-bearer, and Steward, Baron von Mirbach, and the Marshals of the Court, Baron von Reischach and von Trotha—served the soup and the wine to Their Majesties and to us, the bridal pair. This created a somewhat embarrassing situation for us, but it was easily got over with a little kindly humour. The pages waited on us during the rest of the banquet.

During the banquet the Kaiser gave a beautiful address, which touched us deeply. He addressed me as " my dear daughter Cecilie," welcomed me to his House and his family circle in cordial terms, recalled my exalted prototypes, Queen Luise and the other Princesses who had ascended the throne of Prussia, and invoked God's bounteous blessing on our heads. The closing words of this address made the deepest impression on me and I have never forgotten them : " May God and Our Saviour be the foundation of your house ! As His was the supreme personality, whose glorious remembrance has remained with us on earth even to this day, inspiring the hearts of men and leading them to follow in His steps : so may your life too strive to follow His ! Then you will also be con- forming to the laws and traditions of this House. May your household be happy and may it become an example to the young generation, in accordance with the beautiful words which Kaiser Wilhelm der Grosse, as a young man, once set down as his creed : ' My whole being belongs to the world and to the Fatherland ! ' May my blessing go with you on your life's way ! " These words have been as it were a guiding thread in our life together.

The wedding festivities closed with a torch dance in the White Hall. The Crown Prince and I again took our places under the canopy of the throne, between the Kaiser and Kaiserin ; on our left stood the ladies of royal rank, and on our right the Royalties and Princes ; the diplomatic corps and the members of the higher nobility took up their position on a dais opposite to us. The bands began the minuet-like music of the torch-dance, and the Lord Marshal, Count Eulenberg, stepped forward in full uniform and with the Marshal's baton in his hand, followed by twelve pages dressed in red who walked in pairs and with white wax torches in their hands. They halted in front of us, the newly-wedded pair, and bowed. We then opened the dance with a deep obeisance to Their Majesties, and with the Marshal and the twelve pages walking in front of us, we moved as if in a polonaise once round the hall, past the guests, who were standing in close-packed rows. Then I approached the Kaiser, and with a curtsey invited him to dance, while at the same time the Crown Prince invited the Kaiserin. After this there followed in the same manner a third progress round the hall, the Crown Prince with my mother and my brother with me ; and then I danced with each of the four princes, while at the same time the Crown Prince danced with each of the Princesses.

To me, in spite of the wondrous beauty of the scene, whose charm no one who has seen it can ever forget, the ceremony was extremely fatiguing, for my heavy train and the Princesses' Crown were a very considerable weight to carry.

It came to an end at last, and now we moved again in formal procession, and preceded by the pages with their torches, to the bridal chambers, where the crown was with due ceremony removed from my head, and then my Mistress of the Robes, in accordance with ancient custom, cut off the " garter," i.e., a narrow white silk ribbon on which the bride's monogram was inscribed. We then took leave of our nearest relations ; Mama and Miss King helped me to change my dress, and now we could start off on our wedding journey, which was to take us to Hubertusstock in the Schorfheide.

An open victoria took us to the Stettiner station. We felt extremely proud that now, as a married couple, we could drive quite unaccompanied through the streets of Berlin. To our joyful surprise the Kaiser and my brothers-in-law were waiting for us at the station in order to bid us a final farewell. The Kaiser kept up this beautiful custom at all the subsequent marriages of his children. After a cordial leave-taking we got into our new saloon car and travelled to quiet, peaceful Hubertusstock, which my parents-in-law had placed at our disposal for the honeymoon. The Kaiser and Kaiserin were very fond of this little shooting-box, and visited it each year during the autumn. It was very comfortably, though simply furnished, and therefore eminently suited to give hospitable welcome to a young couple.

What a sigh of relief we breathed when, after all those exhausting festivities, we reached the idyllic quiet and solitude of Hubertusstock, to experience there the greatest happiness of our young marriage ! Our hearts filled with deep gratitude to God, who had brought us together.

CHAPTER XII

UP TO MY SILVER WEDDING

It was originally my intention to close this record, so far as it was designed for publication,. with my marriage. But as I gained the impression that it would be better if I showed the conceptions of my childhood and early years in their line of development on wider fields, I decided to deal with the most important aspects of the subsequent period, at least in broad outline.

Twenty-five years lie between the events which have been described and the present day, twenty-five years which have been so rich in events and experiences that this period seems to me to have been almost twice that length.

The first nine years of our marriage passed without a care amid the stream of events of a time of peace and with an untroubled feeling of security based on the strong position of the German Empire. Life at the Prussian Court involved us in many obligations and demanded of us, too, many sacrifices which are not required of other young married couples. But our position made this inevitable, and we had to put up with it. The Crown Prince's military duties made us spend our lives for the most part alternately at Potsdam and Berlin ; the only exception was the two years which we spent at Danzig-Langfuhr when he was in command of the Hussar

Regiment—those were the happiest years of our life !

In the period before the war God sent us four sons, so that my life was richly filled and in this respect was not far different from the lives of other young wives. What a happy moment it was for me when my first-born child was placed in my arms, how indescribably great were the young father's joy and pride in his son and heir, and how the devoted grandmother's face beamed at the auspicious birth of her first grandson ! What hours and days I had of the most intense happiness, which come to every young mother as new and unheard-of experiences ! Blessings of motherhood, which bind us women with our sisters in every walk of life by the tender bands of those inexpressible feelings and experiences which we share in common !

Then came the children's early years, with their cares, their joys and the little happenings of every day : like tiny little stones which will one day form the structure of the completed man. Words are stammered and little signs and indications point to particular characteristics which are present from birth and are waiting development. Likenesses are discovered, prophecies seem to be finding their fulfilment, and from year to year the picture is constantly changing, as younger brothers and sisters join them and the children begin to rub off each other's corners. Often some peculiarity appears which seems to be a defect in the child's character and fills the mother's heart with anxiety for the future ; and then this anxiety is allayed when the rough edges have been worn smooth. What mother does not know the ups and downs of happiness and anxiety which children bring in the early years of anxious care !

And although in other circumstances these little occurrences may pass unheeded within the narrow family circle, in our position, in which even the happenings of the nursery created general interest, they acquired greater importance. For the strong mutual attachment that existed between the nation and the ruling House brought with it a warm interest in whatever happened to the latter even to the smallest detail. Because of this there were many German families in which the little princes, through their descriptions and photographs, were popular in the truest sense of the word.

My time and my strength were almost completely taken up with our family life. And it would necessarily have been so, even if my own inclination had not already limited my activity to this sphere. For my husband and I were almost completely kept away from high politics. But on the other hand the Crown Prince had the weal and woe of his future empire too much at heart for him not to have striven to keep himself fully informed on the tasks which he would one day be called upon to fulfil. He therefore asked his imperial father to allow him some insight into the affairs of government, and, in spite of the severe demands which military service in Prussia imposed even on princes, my husband nevertheless found time to devote himself to political questions in some detail.

As the Crown Prince, in both Prussia and the German Empire, had no rights either in the government or in

administration, his activity in this connection could be
only of an informatory character. In the Lord-Lieu-
tenant's office at Potsdam, at the Ministry of the Interior,
the Ministry of Finance and the Admiralty, my husband
over a long period attended instructive lectures, some
of which were given by the Ministers themselves ; his
work in the Foreign Office was to come later. In this
way, and also through intercourse with politicians of all
parties, in the course of some years he acquired a valuable insight into the affairs of government as well as
into tendencies both abroad and at home. My husband
followed with anxious care the gathering of the political
clouds both at home and abroad which were massing
above the horizon and menacing the strong bulwark of
the Prussian and German monarchy.

As the Crown Prince, because of his unofficial position,
was able in many respects to gain a somewhat deeper
insight into conditions, he always eagerly strove, in spite
of his youth, to inform his imperial father of his impressions, and in this way to help wherever he could. Often,
too, my husband used to express his anxieties and fears
also to me and a few of his intimate friends, so that by
degrees I gained an idea of the political situation existing
at that time, which was menacing enough for Germany.
For the ring was drawing closer and closer about us ;
since 1907-08 the Anglo-Russian Entente had come to
supplement the Franco-Russian Entente, while Germany
could still only count on Austria-Hungary as her ally.
And for that reason, in spite of all the happiness of our
married life, in spite of all the pleasures, such as dancing,

sport and hunting, which are the privilege of all young people who are enjoying life, we were always conscious of the very serious position with which we were faced. It has been my pride that particularly in this sphere I was able to be my husband's confidant. But he held the view, and in this he was right, that his wife must keep herself aloof from any political activity, that she must be nothing less, but at the same time nothing more, than a comrade who was competent to form an opinion. And so in those years I came near to an understanding of the great world constellations through the exchange of ideas and through reading and my own observation, without ever wanting to play the part of a political woman.

I do not desire to go into details here, not even in regard to the year 1908, in which the internal political conflict developed, nor to the year 1911, when difficulties in foreign relations were particularly pronounced. We passed through these storms filled with anxiety, but with a firm faith in the wonderful powers and qualities which the German people had shown since 1871 in its unparalleled development of industry and technique. Our glorious army, our magnificent fleet, and our administration with its unrivalled efficiency, provided, according to human reckoning, the guarantee that our neighbours would not wantonly attack us. And as on the other hand we were far from any lust of conquest, we secretly hoped that we should be spared a world war which had been talked of for years everywhere in Europe.

With joy and pride I followed our economic development, especially the growth of our merchant marine and of our ship-building yards, where ship after ship was laid on the stocks for both our own and foreign companies. I had the good fortune to establish friendly relations with President Heineken of the Norddeutscher Lloyd and Herr Carl Ziese, who owned the Schichau Works at Elbing, and I spent many interesting and instructive hours with these two shrewd and far-seeing men. Both of them planned and worked for the greatness, fame and honour of Germany. And because of this I willingly accepted the invitation from the Norddeutscher Lloyd to christen the steamer *Kronprinzessin Cecilie* at the Vulkan yards in Stettin, and also, later on, the beautiful leviathan *Columbus* at the Schichau yards in Danzig. Both of these ships embodied German industry, German ability and German determination and took these with them across the ocean.

Our voyage to India in 1910–11 greatly enriched our minds, for it gave my husband and myself the ability to see things from a wider horizon than was possible at home. We learnt to appreciate, moreover, from our own observation, the immense resources of the British Empire, but at the same time were able to observe the standing that German efficiency and German initiative had won throughout the world. We were welcomed with great friendliness by the British authorities both during our joint stay in Ceylon and also in Egypt. During the period of his stay in India the Crown Prince was the guest of the Viceroy.

The inevitably long separation from my children was made easier for me by the fact that my parents-in-law had our three sons Wilhelm, Louis-Ferdinand and Hubertus, who was then a year old—Friedrich was born only after this voyage—to stay with them. The Kaiserin watched over her grandchildren with untiring care, and our nurse could not tell us enough of the loving solicitude which both grandparents had shown for their grandchildren. The Kaiser and Kaiserin would often come in the evening to the bedsides of the little ones in order to pray with them and act as substitutes for their parents at that solemn hour. And how I was able to rejoice, on my return, at the progress our children had made during the period of my absence !

My husband derived great satisfaction from his military duties, especially in his post as regimental commander. Experts considered him a good strategist, and he took an active interest in military manœuvres on a large scale. He also showed a sound comprehension of the use of cavalry in accordance with the requirements of the times, and for training with this in view. But he was anything rather than a war-seeking militarist, and to me it is hardly believable that my husband in particular was calumniated in foreign countries as a warmonger. His many intellectual interests in the sphere of literature and the drama as well as his great love of sport in every form, no less than his sense of responsibility, are in themselves sufficient to give the lie to these assertions.

War propaganda has also distorted and sullied in the most hideous manner the image of my dear father-in-law. With his deep Christian piety, his kindliness and his ardent love for his people, the Kaiser never thought of mischievously unchaining war. And moreover what could have caused him wantonly to interrupt the wonderful development of our Fatherland which was making rapid progress under his rule, when Germany was well on the way to win by peaceful means the spiritual dominion of the world?

Anyone who saw at first hand, as I saw, with what unshakable confidence in the maintenance of peace the Kaiser set out on his northern journey at the beginning of July 1914, anyone who saw, as I saw, with what suspense he waited up to the final hours before the outbreak of war for the Tsar of Russia's replies to his telegrams which had been designed to maintain peace, anyone who saw, as I saw, how painful it was to him to give the order for mobilisation, would be unable to understand to his dying day how war propaganda could have succeeded in presenting my father-in-law to the world as responsible for the war ! Never has a greater and more shameful lie been spread through the world, and never has the honour of a great and peace-loving nation been more wantonly defamed than in this accusation, which was then actually upheld in a so-called " Treaty " !

The murder of the heir to the Austrian throne and his spouse on June 28th, 1914 at Serajevo burst into our peaceful life like a bolt from the blue. The news of this regicide stunned us. How understandable it is that the German Kaiser should have taken his stand by the side of his ally, the aged Emperor Franz Joseph, and remained loyal to his murdered friend even beyond the grave ! But in spite of this the government maintained its calm and endeavoured with all its might to localise the conflict between Austria and Serbia. We confidently hoped that the Monarchy of the Danube would obtain the satisfaction to which it was entitled, but that world peace would be maintained. It seemed to us incredible that other monarchs could range themselves alongside of the regicides.

Another four weeks passed before the outbreak of war. The Kaiser set out on his northern journey, and we went to the Baltic coast for our summer stay, first to Zoppet and then to Heiligendamm. In the last week of July the notes and telegrams which preceded the outbreak of the world war followed each other in rapid succession. On July 31st I hurried to Potsdam, where my husband had arrived some days before, and then together we lived through all the phases of those unforgettable decisive days. Even in those critical hours there was nowhere in the Kaiser's entourage any trace of any war-fever or even any war-baiting. Everyone acted with grave deliberation, and as far as the Imperial Chancellor was concerned, he was almost overwhelmed by the consciousness of his heavy responsibility to the Fatherland and the German nation.

After the state of imminent danger of war had been declared at noon on July 31st, we accompanied the Kaiser and Kaiserin to Berlin, and there in the old palace on the Spree passed through those fateful hours of August 1st which preceded mobilisation—still filled with the hope that peace would be maintained. Indeed even after the signing of the mobilisation order we all,

245

including my husband and I, still would not abandon hope, so inconceivable did it seem to us that the statesmen of the other side would not utilise every opening to avoid the catastrophe. Events, and then above all the disclosures of the years after the war, have unfortunately shown how greatly we deceived ourselves in thinking this. The war broke out.

It was now for every German to throw in his whole weight to help the Fatherland. The whole of life seemed to have altered at one blow ; one great aim, one lofty purpose, inspired everyone. Germany rose up as one man and took up arms for the war which had been forced upon her.

The first few days were filled with tremendous jubilation and enthusiastic demonstrations in which the German nation took its united stand behind its Kaiser. In front of our Palace in Unter den Linden an immense throng of patriotic men and women stood day and night, and with their singing literally fetched us out of bed in order, when we appeared at the window, to demonstrate to us their loyalty and affection. How happy we were made in those days by the firm bonds between the nation and its royal House !

After these days had passed and when too the leave-taking of our dear ones who were going to the front was over, especially of my husband, who left us on August 3rd, I set myself to helping my mother-in-law in her work for the care of the wounded.

The Kaiserin allocated to each of her daughters-in-law a number of hospitals which we had to look after.

Those entrusted to my care were the Augusta Hospital, the Garrison Hospital and the auxiliary hospital in the Veterans' Association building in Berlin, the military hospital in Bernau and the convalescent home at Biesenthal. We also placed our castle at Oels at the disposal of the authorities and converted it into a military hospital, which continued in existence until July 1919. In addition to this I established a sewing-room in the Crown Prince's palace where the wives of army and naval officers assembled every day to make bandages and hospital clothing. It would lead me too far if I attempted to relate how rich these four war years were in experiences of every kind, if I attempted to describe how grateful our " field-greys " were when I visited them in my hospitals and tried to give them some little pleasure. Overwhelmed by the inability of any human being to give any real help, I stood at the bedsides of the seriously-wounded who were suffering for Germany.

During the war years I also had the good fortune to establish close personal relations with Frau Dr. Hedwig Heyl. In the early days of August 1914, with the approval of the Kaiserin, she had brought into being the National Women's Service in Berlin, which for several years did good work in the capital. In the course of many talks Frau Heyl gave me a deeper insight into the urgent social tasks of women at that period, and aroused my active interest in all these weighty questions of the present day. She often told me in these talks of the battles which, together with her friend the clever Kaiserin Friedrich, she had waged in former years, and how they had striven to train the German housewife in the practical and useful conduct of her household. I have also to thank Frau Heyl for a series of lectures which were held in the Crown Prince's palace in the course of the last winter of the war. Names such as Gertrud Bäumer, Elizabeth Lüders, Alice Salomon and Anna von Gierke are a sufficient indication of how rich in content were these lectures, at which the Kaiserin also was sometimes present. For my mother-in-law knew, as I did, that in order to understand great social questions more is required than merely a warm and sensitive heart and goodwill : some expert knowledge is absolutely essential. And so both the close personal relations of friendship with Frau Hedwig Heyl, and the contact with all social and important questions, were a great gain in my life.

During the war my mother-in-law was untiring in her visits to hospitals ; she visited innumerable towns through Germany, and she brought consolation and love wherever she went. I know from the mouths of many wounded men that they welcomed the kind Kaiserin's visits as they did those of their own mothers. And she herself had the feeling that they were her children, her wards, to whom she wanted to do good and show her affection out of her overflowing heart.

I shall never forget Pastor Conrad's quiet hours of war prayers in the Kaiser Wilhelm Memorial Church, which my mother-in-law used to attend with me. How that inspired preacher knew how to bring consolation to his congregation, with what powerful words he prayed for strength to hold out, and with what earnestness he warned us that we must fulfil our duties, however hard they might be !

The long war in the trenches succeeded the tempestuous advance of our field-greys during the first summer. More and more enemies arose against us in the world, and at the end no fewer than twenty-nine states were in the field against Germany and its three allies, and more than forty million soldiers of the Entente were fighting against twenty-two million of the Central Powers. My husband was placed in command of the Fifth Army, which fought at Longwy, in the Argonne, in the battle of the Marne and then in Champagne ; in 1916 he was with his troops in the hell of Verdun, and in the following year he took over the command of the Army of the German Crown Prince.

Two daughters, Alexandrine and Cecilie, were born to us during the four years of the war ; they became the sunshine of our house. Owing to the military position my husband was not able to come home for the christening of our little Alexandrine. So I went to visit him at his staff headquarters at Stenay, and there, on the morning of the second day, I experienced a heavy aeroplane attack, although up to then this territory had been spared from air attacks. No fewer than twenty-four aeroplanes bombarded our unprotected house for a space of two hours ; one hundred and sixty bombs were afterwards found. The attack cost the lives of three gallant sentries and a number of civilians in the town, but we ourselves were spared as if by a miracle. Terrible as these hours were, I should not like to be without this experience

249

of the war in my memory. For God had granted it to me
to share with my husband these hours of supreme
danger, and in this way too I had gained some idea,
though admittedly only in a limited form, of the horrors
to which the soldiers at the front were hourly exposed.

Meanwhile at home economic distress was growing,
and there was a shortage of everything. In the first place,
food. Even in our household we imposed great restrictions
on ourselves from the very beginning. The Kaiserin set
a splendid example and forbade at her table everything
that savoured of luxury. But by degrees the distress
increased and became unbearable. The hunger blockade,
like an iron ring, drew ever closer round the Central
Powers. A great shortage of all nutritious foods developed
and a terrible mortality set in among the children. More
than 700,000 of the civilian population fell victims to
the hunger blockade. Everyone of us longed for the end
of the war, but no one who loved his Fatherland lost
confidence in its successful outcome until the autumn of
1918.

The entry of the fresh and splendidly equipped
American troops was fatal to us. And added to this there
was the unrest in our own country. So came about the
most terrible thing that Germany has experienced in its
two-thousand years of history. There came the revolution. There came the armistice. There came finally the
dictated peace of Versailles. These events are so tragic
that it is impossible for me to speak of them even to-day.

I lived through the November days with my mother-
in-law in the new Palace at Potsdam. In my mind's eye

I see her standing there, tall and upright ; she would not let herself be overwhelmed by the weight of events. In her selfless way she did not think of herself ; she thought only of her Germany, of her dear husband and her children. Only once did I hear her sorrowfully lamenting that now she would have to give up her charitable work at the institutions to which she was so much attached, and her duties as the mother of her people.

She was filled with touching concern for me. Owing to her fear that something might happen to my children and myself, she wanted me to leave the disturbed neighbourhood of the capital and to travel with her to Holland where she intended to share her husband's exile. But I would not consent to leave Germany or even Potsdam, for I did not want to abandon the Fatherland just at its darkest hour. Our children must be brought up as Germans, they must grow up in their German home and even in altered relations they must not be estranged from their people. The Kaiserin too appreciated this and went abroad without me. It was with a heavy heart that she took leave of us, and her children and grandchildren. Never again was she to tread the soil of her beloved country.

Things were not the same for my husband as they were for me. As the new Government had refused to allow his further service in the army, there was nothing left for him but to go for a time to a neutral foreign country. So there now came the five years of separation and exile on the Dutch island of Wieringen on the Zuider Zee. I need not say how hard these years were for us in every way. If my husband was able to endure residence on that barren little island, in primitive conditions, without losing his mental elasticity, he owes it only to the hard physical training of his youth and the philosophical outlook on life which he acquired in the course of years and which helped him over many despondencies and embitterments.

The education of the children fell almost entirely on my shoulders, as was the case with so many women during the years of the war. This unnatural state of things then continued for the further long period of my husband's exile at Wieringen. I had in particular to substitute the strong hand of the father in relation to my growing sons, although the mother should by rights assume the rôle of a mediator in the home. I strove to bring up my sons as capable and simple human beings who would one day be able to hold their own as real Germans. Circumstances compelled us to give up the carefully planned private tuition and to let the children attend a state school. And although the teaching was naturally more superficial than if they had been taught at home, it nevertheless had the advantage that from their youth up our sons were brought into contact with the most varied types of people, and by this means learnt to understand other people's ideas and also to make good themselves, which helps to harden one's character. It was quite a different form of education from any previously known at the Prussian Court, but I hope that it too will bear fruit. I recall with gratitude all those who gave me their practical help and counsel in this difficult task.

Our sons are now already all out in the world, and we parents must with infinite gratitude rejoice in their development and in the energetic and purposeful way in which each of them according to his own individuality has embarked on life.

We were able, it is true, to go every year to Wieringen for a few days, but the restricted accommodation in the house made any longer stay impossible. How sad it was for us each time when we had to say farewell and leave our husband and father once again alone on the island ! Our only consolation was the charming way in which the people of Wieringen treated my husband. It was a genuine friendship that linked the Crown Prince with the fishermen. The local officials did all they could to make these difficult years easier for him, and we shall never forget the touching kindness which the Peerebom and Kolff families showed to my husband and also to me when I came there on my visits.

In this period came the severe illness of the Kaiserin and ultimately her death. When I visited her at Doorn for the last time in August, 1920, she already found it so difficult to walk that she had to be wheeled about. She was in deep mourning for her beloved youngest son Joachim, and she looked infinitely delicate and frail. She was as kind and as affectionate as ever, indeed she had grown perhaps even more tender-hearted in her foreign environment. For although Doorn House is comfortable enough and she had her most cherished mementos about her in her rooms, nothing was any use : she and the Kaiser were in exile, in " Elend " (misery) as the Germans used to call it. She suffered grievously at being cut off from her country. When I took my leave of her and my last look fell on her dear form in the doorway of the house, my heart told me that I would never see this devoted mother here on earth again.

During her last winter the Kaiserin suffered from continuous ill-health, until finally her heart stopped beating and her suffering was over. The misfortune of her Fatherland had broken the Kaiserin Auguste Viktoria's heart, as long ago Queen Luise's heart had been broken. But Queen Luise had died among her loyal people as their adored queen, while the Kaiserin died in a foreign land, in exile, having lost her throne and having been cut off from her work and duties as the mother of her people. Truly an appalling fate !

Every German still remembers the last journey home and the interment of the late Kaiserin. The loyalty and affection which were shown at her funeral compensated for a great deal. The wreaths of flowers which are still brought every day to the Old Temple at Potsdam are convincing proof that loyalty is not yet dead in Germany.

Even the five long years at Wieringen ultimately drew to their close, and thanks to the advent of more sensible politicians in Berlin the Crown Prince was able to come back to his home. We once more resumed our family life in Oels and Potsdam, but of course in completely altered circumstances. But even though with heavy hearts we have had to give up many of our obligations, and even though we of the royal family no longer have official status, we have nevertheless gained something of infinite value : simple humanity. We come into contact with people whom circumstances formerly kept at a distance from us, and find grateful pleasure in the loyalty and affection which are shown to us. For we know that whoever is loyal to us now is sincere. And that is a wonderful feeling.

It is our ardent endeavour to serve the Fatherland in any way we can, beyond all political entanglements and all Party strife, and to bring up our children as German men and women. Our future is in God's hands. We place our trust in Him, that He will shape it in such a way as will bring happiness to us and well-being to the Fatherland.

*

Great historical events have wrought such changes in all our lives that I sometimes have the feeling that the years of my youth belonged to the realm of imagination. But even though so much has changed in externals, and even though my mental outlook on many things is now different, I nevertheless believe that the older I get the nearer I come to the essentials of my being.

I am convinced that a human being can only withstand times of stress and general upheaval without damage to his soul, if he remains faithful to himself. That means, only if he retains the personality which forms the basis of his life and develops it to its highest possible expression. This does not debar him from appreciating the good which every period of change brings with it. But there are certain fundamental principles which he must not disavow, or he himself will begin to waver and lose sight of the inner content in the welter of opinions and ideas, until in the end they overwhelm him.

It is from this point of view that I see the events of my life as they unfold themselves before me. Fate has brought events which have broken into and changed the course of my life. Have I succeeded in facing them and reacting to them, with God's help, in such a way that they have been beneficial to me? Is the goal still unchanged in view? These are questions which it may take a whole life's seeking and striving to answer. It is probably granted to very few among us to reach full clarity, and it is a special act of grace if anyone here on earth attains it. How much the more must we strive to test by this decisive question everything that we experience, everything that we undertake. For in the last resort the only thing that matters is how we endure our ordeals and the blows of fate, so that at the end of our lives it may not be said that we were weighed in the balance and found wanting.

Printed in the USA
CPSIA information can be obtained
at www.ICGtesting.com
LVHW011931200424
777980LV00001B/101